D0893375

ROMANTIC PROGRESSION
The Psychology of Literary History

ROMANTIC PROGRESSION
The Psychology of Literary History

COLIN MARTINDALE

Department of Psychology
University of Maine at Orono

PSYCHOLOGY TODAY
LIBRARY

HEMISPHERE PUBLISHING
CORPORATION
Washington, D.C.

A HALSTED PRESS BOOK

JOHN WILEY & SONS

New York   London   Sydney   Toronto

Acknowledgments

Quotation on pages 13-14 from A. E. Housman, *The Name and Nature of Poetry*, New York: Cambridge University Press, 1933, pp. 49-50. Reprinted by permission.

Quotations on pages 33 and 35 from P. Sorokin, *Social and Cultural Dynamics*, abridged version, Boston: Porter Sargent, Publishers, 1957, p. 639. Reprinted by permission.

Quotation on page 54 from C. D. Abbott, *Poets at Work*, New York: Harcourt Brace Jovanovich, 1948, p. 176. Reprinted by permission.

Quotation of Mallarmé's "Crise de vers" on page 78 from A. Hartley (Ed.), *Mallarmé*, London: Penguin Books, Ltd., 1965, pp. 166, 171, 174. Reprinted by permission.

Quotation of Rimbaud's "Lettre du Voyant" on page 80 from O. Bernard (Ed. and trans.), *Rimbaud*, London: Penguin Books, Ltd., 1966, pp. 9-11. Reprinted by permission.

Quotation of Mallarmé's "Hérodiade" on pages 81-82 from W. Fowlie, *Mallarmé*, Chicago: The University of Chicago Press, 1943, p. 145. Copyright in the International Copyright Union. Reprinted by permission.

Quotation of Breton's "Tiki," Eluard's "Nous sommes," and Michaux' "Un Homme paisible" on pages 88 and 89 from W. Fowlie (Ed. and trans.), *Mid-Century French Poets*, New York: Twayne Publishers, Inc., 1955, pp. 169, 191, 193, 243. Reprinted by permission.

Quotation of Char's "Seuil" on page 89 from A. Hartley (Ed.), *The Penguin Book of French Verse*, Vol. 4, *The Twentieth Century*, London: Penguin Books, Ltd., 1959, p. 291. Original French edition, R. Char, *Fureur et mystère*, © Editions Gallimard 1948. Reprinted by permission.

Copyright © 1975 by Hemisphere Publishing Corporation. All rights reserved. No part of this book may be reproduced in any form, by photostat, microform, retrieval system, or any other means, without the prior written permission of the publisher.

Hemisphere Publishing Corporation
1025 Vermont Ave., N.W., Washington, D.C. 20005

Distributed solely by Halsted Press, a Division of John Wiley & Sons, Inc., New York.

Library of Congress Cataloging in Publication Data

Martindale, Colin.
    The Romantic progression.

    Bibliography: p.
    1. Poetics. 2. Creation (Literary, artistic,
etc.) 3. Literature—Psychology. 4. French poetry—
History and criticism. I. Title.
PN1031.M362   808.1   74-26559
ISBN 0-470-57365-1

Printed in the United States of America

CONTENTS

ACKNOWLEDGMENTS

This book has been immeasurably improved as a result of the comments and encouragement of Drs. D. E. Berlyne of the University of Toronto and Irvin Child of Yale University. Discussions with Drs. David McClelland, Henry Murray, Erwin Staub, and Philip Stone of Harvard University, and with Dr. Robert Holt of New York University have also added insights which are incorporated at various points. Drs. Arthur Dempster, Frederick Mosteller, Robert Rosenthal, and Mr. Michael Sutherland of Harvard University provided valuable advice on the statistical aspects of the studies reported in this book, and John Kirsch provided unstinting assistance with the computer aspects of the studies. Special thanks are due to Dr. Lane Conn, who provided encouragement when others were skeptical and often less than encouraging. I owe a special debt of gratitude to Dr. Wallace Fowlie of Duke University, who first interested me in the French literary tradition and in many of the problems confronted in this book. Thanks are also due to Dr. Stanley Pliskoff and Dean John Nolde of the University of Maine for providing facilities and financial assistance for preparation of the manuscript, and to Sharon Smith and Louise Young for typing the final draft. Parts of the research reported in this book were supported by grants 1-F1-MH-30, 452-01 (MTLH) and 5-F1-MH-30, 452-02 (MTLH) from the National Institute of Mental Health.

Part I
A THEORETICAL APPROACH TO LITERARY CHANGE

Chapter 1
INTRODUCTION

La base de l'histoire doit être la psychologie scientifique
TAINE

THE PROBLEM: ARTISTIC CHANGE

Literature and art have, in the twentieth century, undergone bizarre permutations so that they seem but distantly related to what used to be considered beautiful or great. Poetry in particular has exhibited strange metamorphoses. In the early part of the century the surrealists and their predecessors began writing verse which seemed to refer to nothing either inside or outside the spirit of man; "like" no longer joined like things but disparate and unrelated ones. "The earth," said Eluard, "is blue like an orange"; Breton spoke of "seas, red like the egg when it is green." Today, the most avant-garde schools of poetry produce "concrete" poetry wherein letters and words are randomly scattered on a page. In the theater, the absurd reigns supreme, while in painting Pollock's random splashes are treasured in museums.

How have these things come about? How are they connected with the art of preceding centuries? If we look to history, we see that such strange artistic vicissitudes are not confined to the twentieth century. Praz (1933), for example, has shown that sexual roles as portrayed in European literature tended to reverse over the course of the nineteenth century, going from an exacerbation of contemporary cultural roles toward an inversion apparently unsupported by changes in the larger society. In the sixteenth and seventeenth centuries the metaphysical and précieux

3

schools and movements such as Marinism, Gongorism, and euphuism produced poetry which, though often rationalized by classical theories, seemed increasingly to pursue the bizarre and the unnatural.

May not poetry and the other arts sometimes fall, as even the Marxist critic Caudwell was forced to concede, into "poetic pockets" where they follow a logic or destiny of their own so bizarre as to become more a subject for the psychologist than the humanist? But the psychologist, once he has established even such a tenuous claim to the subject, sees that the behavior of art and artists in such autonomous "pockets" constitutes a sort of natural experiment: the scientist, when he seeks to understand an event, examines it in some sort of vacuum. In the social sciences, Weber's method of considering "ideal cases" is a straightforward analogue of Galileo's consideration of falling objects in a vacuum. May it not be that the effect of society upon literary change is the analogue of the effect of mass upon the rate of fall of an object, that by considering literary change in an "unnatural" vacuum we may discover the laws which govern it in general? To carry the analogy forward, we shall attempt to specify the artistic equivalent of gravity and to delineate the psychological laws which govern it.

RELEVANCE OF PSYCHOLOGY
TO THE PROBLEM

It cannot be denied that some of the transmutations which make up the history of poetry are fascinating, but can it not be argued that the construction of any sort of general theory of literary change is beyond the scope of psychological study? Even in strict behavioristic definitions psychology is seen as the study of the behavior of organisms. Poetry is no less the product of such behavior than are the test responses of college sophomores or the bar-presses of rats and pigeons. There is a certain empirical justification for being wary of attempts to bring psychology to bear on "relevant" or "important" issues. The "third force" psychologists who have attempted to do so have often ended by bringing something else than scientific psychology to bear on them, by losing rigor and objectivity. Nothing is gained by a mystical "explanation" of mysticism or sentimental effusions concerning poetry or creativity. It was precisely because Bleuler regarded his patients as stranger than the flowers in his garden, because Freud regarded his as not at all worth saving, that they were able to understand them so well. We intend to offer the poet no special advantage over the laboratory rat: tender-mindedness is entirely a matter of approach, not of subject matter.

Beyond the legitimacy of the subject, if rightly approached, there is a growing theoretical and empirical literature on the psychology of creativity and of aesthetics which has not as yet been systematically applied to the problem of art history. It would be difficult to assert that art is not conditioned by its psychic means of production and by the personalities of its producers. It will be shown that such conditioning is indeed basic to an understanding of literary change.

It might be argued that, even if psychology can legitimately be applied to the problem of literary change, its application will somehow debase the subject of study. At the very least is it not somehow sacrilegious to quantify poetry and vivisect the minds of its creators? One would not drop a jeweled Fabergé egg in order to see whether it conformed to the laws of gravity, but John Belter, the nineteenth-century furniture maker, did keep several of his best chairs in his second-floor office precisely for tossing out of his window in order to prove their durability. Moreover, the scientific study of literature is mute about the usual concerns of literary critics: it cannot and should not say anything regarding the absolute quality of works.

PREVIOUS APPROACHES TO THE PROBLEM

We see that a psychological approach to the problem of literary change is legitimate, may be fruitful, and neither debases the object of study nor usurps it from other disciplines. But is there a need for such an approach? Are the phenomena not sufficiently explained by already existing theories? Let us examine briefly the several species of existing theories to see whether they are complete and convincing. Perhaps the most common approach to art stems from the assumption that art reflects the "spirit of the age"—the *Zeitgeist*, or dominant cultural orientation of a society. Given this, changes in art can be referred to changes in this spirit. The approach is based upon Hegel's (1835) philosophy of spirit and upon de Stael's (1800) maxim that "literature is the reflection of society." Examples of the approach are the correlation of baroque forms with a sense of power and Gothic ones with spiritual agitation. The approach is so imbued into our thinking that its weaknesses are overlooked. The problem of how to determine the spirit of an age is a massive one. As Schücking (1923) points out, "The spirit of the Gothic period . . . is first deduced from its art and then rediscovered in its art." Even if one were able to confine his determination of the cultural *Zeitgeist* to wholly extra-artistic data, the problem of how to measure such elusive phenomena with any degree of precision remains. Henry Murray once asked me to specify the dominant force characterizing Western civilization since the Middle Ages. My reply centered on conquest and Faustian striving. Murray, his rhetorical question ruined, replied that he had hoped I would say that it was decay and degeneration. We had offered diametrically opposed solutions and there was no way of determining who was correct.

Styles exhibit different rates of change in different arts. Brunetière (1894), Combarieu (1913), and Sorokin (1937) have documented the tendency of music to lag behind other arts. In the various arts, different styles must, then, coexist at the same time. Such styles cannot all derive from the same *Zeitgeist*. This opens the way for questioning whether *any* of them are so derived. *Zeitgeist* theorists imply a filtering of values from the most abstract and general orientations of a culture to the lower and more concrete level of artistic products. Even if we grant that such an influence exists, there is usually no thought given to the *mechanisms* whereby the influence occurs. Rather, a sort of action by sympathy is invoked. Finally, since such theories attempt to correlate phenomena of quite divergent types, only very general and vague correspondences may be expected.

This approximateness of correspondence can be partially attributed to inertial and self-energizing factors possessed by different social systems. Perhaps the key lies with these properties; perhaps change in systems of art is largely independent of change in the larger society. Such theories of immanent change have been espoused by those who have followed Wölfflin (1888) and Riegl (1901). Both saw art as changing mainly in response to intra-systemic factors—the latter to the desire to represent reality and the former to changes in perception. A number of theorists (Chambers, 1928; Deonna, 1912; Kroeber, 1944; Michaud, 1950) have espoused cyclical theories of art history which see the latter as following an internally determined pattern of growth, flowering, and decay: they claim that, unless violently disrupted by external influences, any artistic tradition approximates such cycles. Foçillon (1942) and Fiedler (1949) have discussed art history in terms of the working out of the possibilities inherent in stylistic forms. Such theories have fallen out of fashion for several reasons. Those based upon qualitative cycles of growth, flowering, and decay are made suspect by the tendency to rehabilitate styles formerly seen as decadent. The rediscovery of beauty in baroque forms in the 1920's and in mannerist ones in the 1950's make it all too clear that aesthetic quality is not a stable basis for theory building. Theories of the working out of inherent possibilities of forms, of an inner logic to historical succession, of the impossibility of work B without work A are weak in that the "what" and the "why" are often not clearly specified: *what* exactly is the inner logic? *why* could Mallarmé, say, not have written what he did before Baudelaire wrote what he did? These specifications cannot be made primarily because the psychological and sociological mechanisms mediating the changes are not made explicit: forms cannot change of themselves but are changed by virtue of the operation of psychological laws governing their producers.

That there is, however, something to the immanent approach is illustrated by Nordau's (1895, p. 539) description of the poetry of the future: "Books such as those of the present day have not been in fashion for a very long time. Printing is now only on black, blue, or golden paper, on another colour are single incoherent words, often nothing but syllables, nay, even letters or numbers only." From the trend of the art of his day, Nordau anticipated the concrete poetry of ours. Predictions are rare in art history and this one is as striking as the phenomena it predicts; knowing nothing of world wars or "ages of anxiety" and "alienation," Nordau was able to make a nonobvious prediction about the future.

Intermediate between *Zeitgeist* and immanent-change theories are the diffusion theories often espoused by those who restrict themselves to the history of only one art. For example, a link is often drawn between irrationalism in philosophy and science (e.g., Nietzsche, Bergson, Freud, Heisenberg) and the chaos of modern art. Certainly the boundaries between the arts are permeable, but diffusion explains little. At most, as Gide has said, "influence creates nothing; it awakens something."

These approaches lack a basis in systematic psychology or sociology. Let us turn for a moment to theories based upon these disciplines. Purely psychological approaches to artistic change are rare. The most common base their explanations upon satiation or boredom with old styles. However, such explanations are inadequate because they can only account for changes within the lifetime of a single generation. Clearly, boredom cannot cumulate across generations. One must assume some sort of implicit and, therefore, probably inadequate sociological model or else get into even worse difficulties. Ehrenzweig (1953), for example, falls into Lamarckian speculations in order to provide a bridging device across generations for a purely psychological theory of artistic change. Another sort of psychological theory avoids the problem of generational gaps in seeing changes in art as being due to the natural evolution of consciousness. Neumann (1954) explains changes in mythic content and Kahler (1973) changes in European narrative in terms of man's increasing powers of abstraction and analysis. While these authors make a fascinating and internally consistent case for their theories, their only real evidence for them is the changes in art which they set out to explain in the first place.

Modern sociological approaches to art have succeeded best where they have involved the analysis of the social condition of the artist (e.g., analysis of the artistic subculture in terms of roles, norms, institutions, and interchanges with other social organizations). Schücking (1923) has produced perhaps the classical study in this respect. He avoids the mistakes of trying to reduce artistic change more or less entirely to larger social causes on the one hand, and of trying to derive psychological facts from sociological ones on the other. Marxist theorists such as Plekhanov (1913) and Lukács (1964) offer cogent analyses of changes in the social position of the modern writer, but they often attempt to derive changes in literary content directly or with reference only to an implicit psychology from such social changes. If, as will be argued, the two sets of social facts are in reality mediated by something other than such a psychology, by altered states of consciousness rather than by ordinary and familiar ones, then this sort of explanation is bound to run into difficulties. An explanation of the modern artist's "loss of reality" solely in terms of his social alienation could be convincing only if one believed in the first place that reality were determined by class perspective alone. Even the Marxist would have to admit, though, that class perspective could influence one's grasp of reality only via perceptual, cognitive, and other psychological mechanisms and that these mechanisms are influenced by other factors besides social class. Plekhanov (1913) has attempted to explain the modern poet's tendency to hate bourgeois values. It is not unfair to summarize his answer as being that bourgeois society is *in fact* hateful. Even on the sociological level the question is framed in an unfruitful manner; one ought not to ask why artists hate the middle class but rather why those recruited (largely from the middle class) as artists tend to hate it.

But this done, one is confronted with the need for an explicit psychology and with the possibility that only certain personality types are recruited to fill the role of artist; given this possibility, it is not safe to try to get by with an implicit, common-sense psychology.

Much modern sociology of art and literature (e.g., Albrecht, 1956; Hauser, 1951; Kavolis, 1968) continues the idea that art on some level reflects social values or structures. Such approaches differ from *Zeitgeist* theories in that they tend to derive aesthetic phenomena "from below"—from material culture—rather than "from above." Often, unfortunately, in Gombrich's (1953) felicitous phrasing, such "sociological explanations really turn out to be psychological fallacies." Kavolis (1968, pp. 24 and 193), for example, attempts to find a mechanism for this reflection or correspondence in the psychological need for congruence or consonance between attitudes toward art forms and toward social structures. But there is direct evidence that creative subjects are less affected by this need than are people in general (Martindale, Abrams, and Hines, 1974) and indirect evidence that they may even prefer dissonance and incongruity.

What might be called the "modern condition" theory seeks to derive modern literary changes from increasing social complexity, disorganization, decay of values, and anomie. There is a parallel hypothesis in the field of psychiatric epidemiology: that these social conditions have led to increases in mental illness in the same time period. Both hypotheses are based upon the implicit assumption that complexity and rapid social changes impose increasingly unbearable psychic stresses upon the individual. The epidemiological question has been put to the test a number of times. The increases over time that are found seem best ascribed to such artifacts as changing definitions of mental illness and increased availability of mental hospitals (see Dunham, 1968). It seems probable that modern stresses are merely different from, rather than more intense than, historical ones. Again, the proposed psychological mechanism seems to be inadequate.

Although larger social changes may condition literary history, one cannot claim to have explained their effects until he has specified the *mechanisms* whereby this effect is generated. Any explanation must consist of a deduction of what is to be explained from a specification of initial conditions and from a specification of a general law or set of laws (cf. Hempel and Oppenheim, 1948). Saying simply that the modern breakdown of tradition has led to disintegration of poetic form is the equivalent of saying that carrying an object to the top of a building causes it to fall to the ground; it involves a confusion of initial conditions and general laws. An example makes clear the level at which such conditioning may occur. In 1721, a law was passed for the English ship-building trade; it allowed the importation of large quantities of mahogany into England. An altogether unforeseen consequence was furniture makers' changing from use of native woods to mahogany as their chief material. This change, mahogany being a very strong wood, facilitated or allowed the elaborate rococo productions of the later years of the century. Clearly, the law did not *cause* this change. Changes in the larger society, whether on the level of *Zeitgeist*, social structure, or material culture, can facilitate or hinder trends in art but they cannot cause them directly.

Perhaps the most important difficulty with all the theories discussed is their lack of specification of *mechanisms* at all levels. Purely psychological theories lack the mechanisms provided by social institutions for extending their explanations across generations. Sociological approaches, on the other hand, tend to rely upon an implicit, common-sense psychology which may apply to the modal personality of a culture but not to its artists. Similarly, immanent-change and *Zeitgeist* theories generally take no consideration of mediating variables, but tend to rely upon "action at a distance" and analogical equilibration.

A PSYCHOLOGICAL THEORY

In this book, we shall develop and support a theory of artistic change which is couched in quantitative rather than qualitative terms, one which deals, on the level of artistic products, not with excellence, but with frequencies and which treats, on the level of creators and audiences, not with the "human spirit" or other inchoate psychic processes, but with the constructs of scientific psychology. The theory will involve an attempt at specification of *mechanisms* of causation: within a systematic sociological framework for the provision of historical continuity, explanation of changes in artistic form and content and in the role of artist will be derived from changes in psychological processes. Although the theory is relevant to art and literature in general, it is worked out in detail only for the case of poetry.

One cannot hope to explain the dynamics of a phenomenon unless he understands its static properties. Consequently, the next two chapters present a set of models concerning various aspects of the creation of artistic products which are taken as axiomatic in the theory of artistic change. Chapter 4 presents the psychological theory of literary change. What is said there is relatively simple: whatever else it must be, a work of art must be more original than previous productions. As the autonomy of a poetic subculture increases, the "whatever elses" (which may have more or less completely suppressed the originality constraint) fade away: The poet experiences a stronger pressure toward novelty and his audience exerts a lessened resistance to it. When this initial originality condition is articulated with the psychological laws governing the production of original responses, we are able to derive predictions concerning the course over time of a number of variables (such as poetic content) not directly predictable from the mere constraint for originality. It is argued that on a number of occasions poetry has indeed been autonomous enough for the theory to constitute a major explanatory tool.

A basic objection to the competing theories reviewed in this chapter is that they are seldom supported by any sort of systematic empirical evidence: proof is by example; there is no attempt to define the population of interest or to sample from it in an objective manner; there is no effort at quantification of variables. The remainder of the book represents attempts, at two levels of control, to provide empirical evidence for the psychological theory of literary change. Chapter 5 provides qualitative support for the theory by an examination of the history of French poetry from 1800 to 1940. The aim here is as much to give the reader a clinical "feel" for the extremely interesting and strange course of this history, to show that there are things here worthy of the psychologist's attention and efforts at explanation, as to demonstrate that the theory can offer comprehensive explanations of these changes. Chapter 6 deals with qualitative applications of the theory to several other contexts. Chapters 7–14 report on a computerized content analytic study of randomly selected texts from twenty-one objectively selected French poets covering the period 1800–1940 and twenty-one objectively selected English poets writing between 1700 and 1840. The two populations were chosen so that one high-autonomy and one low-autonomy series would be available for testing of hypotheses derived from the theory.

Chapter 2
THE CREATIVE PROCESS

A great poet is a man who, in his waking state, is able to do what the rest of us do in our dreams.
SCHOPENHAUER

THE DATA TO BE EXPLAINED

Artists' self-reports tend to divide the creative process into initial inspiration or insight and subsequent working-over of the "given" elements. Concomitant changes in affect, perception, state of consciousness, and cognition are often reported (see Ghiselin, 1952, and Harding, 1940). A few quotes will show that the process of creation is fundamentally different from usual thought processes. Housman's (1933) description of the composition of a poem is particularly clear:

> In short I think that the production of poetry, in its first stage, is less an active than a passive and involuntary process. . . .
> Having drunk a pint of beer at luncheon—beer is a sedative to the brain, and my afternoons are the least intellectual portion of my life—I would go out for a walk of two or three hours. As I went along, thinking of nothing in particular, only looking at things around me and following the progress of the seasons, there would flow into my mind, with sudden and unaccountable emotion, sometimes a line or two of verse, sometimes a whole stanza at once, accompanied, not preceded, by a vague notion of the poem which they were destined to form part of. Then there would usually be a lull of an hour or so, then perhaps the spring would bubble up again. I say bubble up, because, so far as I could make out, the source of the suggestions thus proffered to the brain was an abyss which I have

13

already had occasion to mention, the pit of the stomach. When I got home I wrote them down, leaving gaps, and hoping that further inspiration might be forthcoming another day. Sometimes it was, if I took my walks in a receptive and expectant frame of mind; but sometimes the poem had to be taken in hand and completed by the brain, which was apt to be a matter of trouble and anxiety, involving trial and disappointment, and sometimes ending in failure.

Dryden, in his Dedication to "The Rival-Ladies"[1] puts more emphasis upon elaboration but clearly notes the initial inspirational phase:

And, I confess, in that first tumult of my thoughts, there appeared a disorderly kind of beauty in some of them, which gave me hope, something... might be drawn from them: But I was then in that eagerness of imagination, which, by overpleasing fanciful men, flatters them into the danger of writing; so that when I had moulded it into that shape it now bears, I looked with such disgust upon it, that the censures of our severest critics are charitable to what I thought. ... For imagination in a poet is a faculty so wild and lawless, that, like a high-ranging spaniel, it must have clogs tied to it, lest it outrun the judgment.

The brothers Schlegel, in *The Atheneum*[2] set forth a similar viewpoint: "The beginning of all poetry is to suspend the course and the laws of rationally thinking reason, and to transport us again into the lovely vagaries of fancy and the primitive chaos of human nature." Baudelaire (1859-66, p. 1271) makes the same point symbolically when he speaks "of the vaporization and of the centralization of the *Self*." Blake's (1803) comments on the composition of his poem on Milton are more explicit: "I have written this poem from immediate dictation ... without premeditation, and even against my will." Even Thackeray[3] felt the same possession: "I have been surprised at the observations made by some of my characters. It was as if an occult power was moving the pen." That not merely literary creation is derived from such processes is suggested by Nietzsche's description[4] of the composition of *Thus Spake Zarathustra*: "Everything occurs quite without volition, as if in an eruption of freedom, independence, power and divinity. The spontaneity of the images and similes is most remarkable; one loses all perception of what is imagery and

---

[1] Quoted by Ghiselin (1952).
[2] Quoted by Nordau (1895, p. 73).
[3] Quoted by Harding (1940).
[4] Quoted by Ghiselin (1952).

simile. . . . If I may recall a phrase of Zarathustra's it actually seems as if the things came to one and offered themselves as similes." Poincaré's (1913) often quoted description of the discovery of a class of Fuchsian functions is altogether similar to this: "Ideas rose in crowds; I felt them collide until pairs interlocked, so to speak, making a stable combination. . . . I had only to write out the results, which took but a few hours." It is not only the poet who, in Cocteau's phrase "is at the disposal of his night," who "must clean house and await its due visitation."[5]

FORMULATION CONCERNING THE CREATIVE PROCESS

Historically, there have been two approaches to creativity. One, first articulated by Plato, stresses the role of inspiration and "divine madness," while the other, elaborated by Aristotle, stresses the formal, imitative aspects of the creative process. Nietzsche (1872) synthesized these two approaches to the creative process by proposing that the latter consists of a Dionysian phase followed by an Apollonian one. The Dionysian trance involves a destruction of boundaries between self and others and a loss of the self in the world, the loss of everyday rules and order, and primitive states of rapture and transport. Its analogue is intoxication and its guiding principle is unity as opposed to Apollonian separation and analysis. The Apollonian phase of creation is seen as involving individuation: a tendency to order and understand, to give form and structure.

Modern views of the creative process are analogous to Nietzsche's. Kris' (1952) formulation of the psychoanalytic theory of creation rests upon his concept of "regression in the service of the ego." The latter entails the momentary use of primary process mentation (the sort of thought found in dreaming and in psychosis). According to Kris, regression in the service of the ego corresponds to the inspirational stage of creation; it is followed by elaboration of the creative product using logical or secondary process mechanisms of thought. Empirical work with creative subjects supports the idea that they have readier access to primitive modes of thought than do people in general (Fitzgerald, 1966; Gamble and Kellner, 1968; Hines and Martindale, 1973a; Pine and Holt, 1960; Wild, 1965). Inspiration and elaboration may

[5] Quoted by Ghiselin (1952).

theoretically occur at any points on the primary process-secondary process continuum. There is a good deal of fluctuation back and forth in composing a poem, but we assume that a poem tends to be inspired at a "mean" level and elaborated at another "mean" level. Regression facilitates inspiration since primary process thought, being free-associative and "chaotic," increases the probability of novel combinations of ideas. Without in any way subscribing to other aspects of psychoanalytic theory, we take this as our working model of the creative process.

REGRESSION AND "MENTAL LEVELS"

A number of theorists have held that states of consciousness may be arrayed along a continuum ranging from primitive to advanced. In addition to Freud's (1900) primary process versus secondary process dichotomy, some of the more well known divisions are Lévy-Bruhl's (1910) prelogical versus scientific thinking; Cassirer's (1925) mythic versus rational mode; Goldstein's (1939) concrete versus abstract attitude; Werner's (1948) dedifferentiated or syncretic versus differentiated thought; Mc-Kellar's (1957) A-thinking versus R-thinking; Maslow's (1957) B-cognition versus A-cognition; Berlyne's (1965) autistic versus directed thinking; Neisser's (1967) preattentive processes versus focal attention; Bogen's (1969) appositional versus propositional thought; and Klinger's (1971) respondent versus operant sequencing. I shall use the terms *primary process* and *secondary process* as referring to the hypothetically unitary dimension delineated by all of these theorists. In using Freud's terms for this continuum, I do not mean to accept his hypotheses that primary process thought is related to repression, wish-fulfillment, the unconscious, and the like. Rather, I use the terms only as convenient labels for different types of cognition and perception; indeed, my conception of the continuum is much closer to that of Werner and some of the later writers listed above than to that of Freud.

By *regression* we mean an alteration in state of consciousness entailing a movement toward archaic, undifferentiated modes of thought and perception. Such movement hypothetically occurs in states associated with phenomena as seemingly diverse as dreaming (Freud, 1900), wit (Freud, 1905), slips of the tongue (Freud, 1904), hypnosis (Gill and Brenman, 1959), mystical experiences (Silberer, 1912), alchemical experiments (Jung, 1944, 1956), hallucinogenic drugs (Ludwig, 1969), psychoanalytic psychotherapy (Fenichel, 1945), primitive magic (Roheim, 1955, Werner, 1948), psychosis and neurosis (Fenichel, 1945), brain damage (Goldstein, 1939), and sensory deprivation (Solomon et al., 1961). Development, or the opposite of regression, has been seen primarily in the movement from childhood to adult thought (Piaget, 1950; Werner, 1948), from primitive to civilized thought (Lévy-Bruhl, 1910; Werner, 1948), and from hypnagogic states through reverie and fantasy to normal, waking consciousness (Rapaport, 1957). In a sense, then, creative inspiration finds its analogue in each of these regressed states.

Our basic model is that there is a continuum of *potential* states of consciousness and related modes of "apprehension" ranging from outward-oriented, abstract, problem-solving, secondary process states to primary process, free-associative, reverie-like ones. What changes as we go from the secondary process to the primary process end of the continuum is the mode by which mental contents are apprehended or objectified and the operations by which they are manipulated. The basic characteristic of regressive thought is dedifferentiation (Werner, 1948). Lack of differentiation between perceptual and emotional systems leads to physiognomic or animistic perception; between different perceptual systems to synaesthesia; between succession and causality to *post hoc ergo propter hoc* reasoning; between sign and object to sympathetic magical thought; between part and whole to *pars pro toto* logic and contagious magic; between thought and reality to wish-fulfilling fantasies; between different concepts to diffuse and syncretic ideas; between similarity and identity to analogical thought; between self and world to oceanic, mystical states; and between truth and falsehood to tolerance of contradiction. Secondary process cognition is oriented toward external reality and emphasizes problem solving, abstraction, and analysis, while primary process cognition is autistic, concrete, and features analogical thought employing such devices as symbolization, displacement, and substitution. Attention in secondary process states is focused, while it is unfocused, hazy, and diffuse in primary process states. On the level of phenomenology, primary process states involve decreases in memorability and feelings of volition, derangements in body sense and sense of time and identity, and an upsurge of feelings of rejuvenation and of the ineffable.

State of consciousness may be seen as being based upon level of general cortical activation or arousal (cf. Blum, 1961; Fischer, 1971; Lindsley, 1960; Martindale, 1972b). Secondary process cognition hypothetically accompanies medium levels of arousal, while primary process cognition accompanies either high (as in anxiety or panic and certain drug states) or low (as in drowsiness and meditation) levels of arousal. Given this, we should expect creative inspiration to be dependent upon level of arousal. Indeed, using normal subjects, Martindale and Greenough (1973) found that increases in arousal produced decrements on several tests of creativity. Conversely, creative subjects have been found to operate at lower levels of cortical arousal (in relation to their basal level) than uncreative subjects while taking tests of creativity (Martindale and Hines, 1973a) and when asked to produce associative speech (Hines and Martindale, 1973a). Instructing subjects to be original produces decreased cortical arousal in creative but not in uncreative subjects (Martindale, Hasenfus, and Kinney, unpublished). Consonant with the spontaneous or uncontrolled nature of artistic inspiration, these effects do not seem to be due to purposive control on the part of the subjects: no differences have been found in the ability of creative and noncreative subjects at biofeedback tasks involving self-control of brain waves (Hines and Martindale, 1973b; Martindale and Armstrong, 1974). As we shall see in the following chapters, variations in level of arousal are as important in determining the reception of the work of art as in its conception.

Chapter 3
THE CREATIVE PRODUCT

Oh, to vex me, contraryes meet in one.
DONNE

SURFACE CHARACTERISTICS

Content

If we were correct in our formulations regarding the creative process, we should expect to find the marks of regression on the creative product. Were there no such marks, were the psychic means of production not to condition the product, its study would be of little value. There is indeed a great deal of evidence that art does reflect its regressive origins. Ehrenzweig (1967) argues that the "minimal content" of any work of art is some residue, or unwitting symbolization of its mode of production. Shumaker (1960) has provided us with a detailed cataloguing of the ubiquity of regressive content in literature. It is obvious, at least, that poetry has usually avoided the sort of secondary process content which is manifest in, say, scientific prose. Further, inspiration at different levels of regresssion seems to show itself with different contents. Since this will be discussed in detail later, it will not be dealt with further at this point. As with dreams (cf. Freud, 1900), one might make a distinction between manifest and latent poetic content. However, we shall ignore this difference since we are interested in broad content categories rather than gradations within these categories owing to elaborational transmutations: to be sure, the poet may, during the elaborational phase, change the associative inspiration (e.g., "green trees' seen sheen") into some cognate statement (e.g., "I saw the oak's green flicker") but he cannot change it into a fundamentally different statement (e.g., "there are flaws in Keynesian economic theory"). Perhaps the most important connotative dimension along which poetic content can vary is that from deep regressive to secondary process images.

Form

By poetic form we understand those structural properties, such as rhythm, rhyme, and syntactic structure, which are independent of content. Syntax corresponds with similar structures in all expressed thought products while rhythm and rhyme are examples of the "artificial" rules which distinguish poetry from prose. In poetic elaboration free-associative chains of elements are automatically transmuted into hierarchically organized, grammatical sentences. The final product, however, seems generally to retain a degree of grammaticality lower than that of prose. Using passages of varying degrees of approximation to English (Miller and Selfridge, 1950), Martindale (1974a) found a strong negative correlation between ratings of "poeticality" and approximation to English. There was a curvilinear component to the relationship, with third-order approximations most preferred, and a slight decline for lower orders of approximation. Regressive form is *automatically* changed as one changes psychic levels. Regressive content may be changed from image to word, but it tends to retain its identity in a way which is impossible for formal aspects: the regressive "syntax" of thought is *lost* during elaboration while regressive content is merely *transmuted*. This is reflected in the traditional psychoanalytic (cf. Freud, 1908; Holland, 1968) treatment of form as adhering closely to the process of elaboration.

Relationship to the Creative Process

The Freudians see inspiration as producing a wish-fulfilling fantasy and elaboration as serving a defensive, distorting, and disguising purpose that makes the work socially acceptable. Our approach is structural or nondynamic and our basic analogue is not the neurotic symptom but the process of linguistic translation. Inspiration produces discourse, which may or may not have wish-fulfilling aspects, on a primary process level. Elaboration involves the translation of this discourse into a more secondary process "language." The purpose of this translation is not defensive but involves the necessity for communication with an audience. Figuratively, poetry resembles not an adult's paraphrase of a child's speech but, since archaic form and content still remain, a paraphrase by a somewhat older child. Elaborational translation changes the "rough draft" of the inspirational phase for the same reasons that translation from, say, German to English changes a text: the lexicon and syntax of the languages differ. As indicated, we assume that translation between any two mental levels involves greater disruptions on the syntactic than on the lexical level.

We assume, then, that the form of a work of art is largely a function of the level at which elaboration occurred. On the other hand, we assume that the content of a work of art approximately reflects its point of regressive origin. While level of elaboration ought theoretically to be seen as a continuum, let us for convenience define four levels or ranges of stylistic elaboration according to whether such elaboration occurs more toward the secondary process or the primary process pole. Together with an example of how an inspirational content ("table"–"chair") might be elaborated, the stylistic levels are:

1. Discursive: Here elaboration is at a high secondary process level. Elements are related in a logical, reality-oriented way with emphasis on rationality, problem solving, and communication. At this level untrue, irrelevant, or absurd statements would be deleted during elaboration. The original juxtaposition is wrenched apart and used in discursive and prosaic fashion (e.g., "I sat on a chair pulled close to the table").

2. Analogical: Elements are compared with some reference to logic and reality (e.g., "a table is like a chair"), but, analogical thought being more regressive than discursive, elaboration is somewhat less stringent. One would expect structure to be less complex and less oriented toward communication.

3. Equational: The elements are equated with relatively little reference to reality (e.g., "tables are chairs"). At this level, thought resembles the transmutations of dreams: different objects are indiscriminantly identified. Syntax should be loose and free-associative.

4. Juxtapositional: The elements are simply juxtaposed in a parataxic manner (e.g., "table chair" or "table and chair" or "chable"). Elaboration is minimal, and the creative product is

chaotic and consists of juxtapositions and fusions of words and phrases with no reference to the rules of syntax, semantics, or reality.

As one goes from level 1 to level 4, interest in communication, logic, meaning, and truth decreases. Adherence to the rules of syntax decreases and structure approaches that found in states of delirium. Degree of approximation to natural language (cf. Miller and Selfridge, 1950) or degree of grammaticalness (cf. Chomsky, 1961) decreases. The levels of elaboration are, however, to be seen as independent of the level from which the inspired content derives. Thus, content derived from any depth of regression can theoretically be elaborated at any of the stylistic levels. Figure 3.1 presents a typology of types of poems based upon these possibilities. In cell 1 of Figure 3.1, we would place neoclassic poetry: inspiration tends to be played down and a large number of rules assure a high degree of elaboration. Content tends to refer to emotions and ideas. In cell 2, certain decadent and symbolic poetry could be placed: in poets such as Mallarmé and Swinburne, content tends to be regressive, referring to drives and sensations with little reference to abstract ideas, but there is a great deal of elaboration, with sonnet forms and other difficult metric systems being employed. Surreal poetry belongs in cell 3: it is not so much regressive as unelaborated. In cell 4, one might place some (nonpoetic) schizophrenic verbalization: elaboration is slight and there is a regressive tone to content.

COLLATIVE CHARACTERISTICS

Traditional aesthetic theories have tended to lean toward a stress on order, beauty, and harmony; but there has been a growing tendency to emphasize incongruity, irregularity, and ambiguity as basic to the arts (e.g., Eliot, 1932; Empson, 1930; Kaplan and Kris, 1948; Meyer, 1956; Peckham, 1965; Read, 1936; and Venturi, 1966). Berlyne (1960, 1971) has discussed art in terms of what he terms *collative variables*: ambiguity, incongruity, complexity, and novelty. These properties are on a level different from form or content. They imply an act of perceiving either formal or contentual inputs in terms of expectational sets. Attention is shifted from the input itself to its apprehension; and, thus, to such higher-level affects as surprise and satisfaction stemming from congruity or incongruity of expectation and reality.

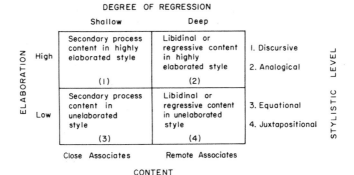

FIGURE 3.1 Relationships among regression/content and elaboration/style.

Metaphor Distance

Consider the following passage from Apollinaire's "Zone."

Here even the automobiles have the air of being ancient
Religion alone has remained completely new religion
Has remained simple like the hangars at the airfield

The immediately striking thing about the passage is its surprisingness, its various improbabilities. Some of the *content* (automobiles, airfield hangars) may be relatively novel—if one judges the piece from a nineteenth-century perspective—in that it is "unpoetic." Also, the *form* is surprising in that punctuation and capitalization are omitted. But, what one cannot escape are the semantic juxtapositions "automobiles"-"old" and, especially, "religion"-"hangars." Theoretically we could arrive at some estimate of the probability of this patch of text appearing when and where it did. The probability would depend upon the elements employed, their structural articulation, and their meaning. Thus, the statement regarding religion's simplicity is less probable than the statement "religion has grown complex like its cathedrals," but more probable than "religion old being of air the have automobiles the even here."

Let us define *metaphor distance* as the relative dissonance of a "patch" of poetic text. On the objective level this refers to the probability of the occurrence of the elements in the text in the manner in which they occur. On the level of expectations, it is roughly proportional to the degree of surprise they engender. Metaphor distance is an inverse function of overlap in (denotative and connotative) meanings and a direct function of the degree of incongruity in such meanings between two elements. Metaphor distance is of primary interest in metaphors and similes where two discrete elements or ideas are involved, but elements juxtaposed in their inspirational origins may be wrenched away from direct comparison during the process of elaboration. Thus, metaphor distance must be defined as referring to juxtapositions in general rather than only to explicit comparisons.

Examples of low metaphor distance statements would be such commonplaces as "lips red like wine," or "rosy cheeks." Higher metaphor distance is evinced by what Wells (1924) labeled the *radical image*: "Radical imagery occurs where two terms of a metaphor meet on a limited ground and are otherwise definitely incongruent." Some examples are:

> Christ left his grave-clothes that we might, when grief
> Draws tears or blood, not want an handkerchief.
> > *G. Herbert*, "Dawning"

> Call her the Metaphysics of her sex
> And say she tortures wit as quartans vex
> Physicians; call her the square circle; say
> She is the very rule of Algebra.
> > *J. Cleveland*
> > "The Hecatomb to his Mistress"

Even greater metaphor distance adheres to poetic statements, such as Eluard's "The earth blue like an orange," which are more or less completely incongruous.

Metaphor Distance and the Creative Process

Metaphor distance should be a function of depth of regression. Holding level of stylistic elaboration constant, deeper regression will produce images of greater metaphor distance since regression increases the probability of juxtapositions of remote associates. On the other hand, metaphor distance should also be an inverse function of degree of elaboration. Holding depth of regression constant, lower levels of stylistic elaboration will produce images of greater metaphor distance since lowering elaboration lessens the stringency of rules governing the appropriateness of poetic combinations. These two determinants of metaphor distance do not, however, have equal weight. Rather, level of elaboration would seem to be the more important. Consider the statement, "the table is food for the chair." Here we have juxtaposed with *table* the two words that are most likely when *table* is used as a stimulus word in word association tests (Russell and Jenkins, 1954). However, we have obtained an original and, in modern poetic practice, a creative (i.e., original *and* acceptable or useful) image. The statement was not produced by deep regression, but it did require a temporary abrogation of the rules of good sense. In other words, it is a product of *low* regression and *low* elaboration. Elaboration governs the conceptual similarity of frames of reference brought together by free-associative or regressive thought (where mental contents are organized by principles such as contiguity and sound similarity rather than by conceptual similarity). Metaphor distance is, then, a joint function of associative probability and conceptual similarity, with the latter contributing more weight. Many very original metaphors and images are purloined letters, continually at the tips of our tongues but never uttered. Since the poet originally derives his statements in an associative manner, he may, if he moves to a lower range of elaboration reap a sort of "poetic dividend." Juxtapositions of close associates, requiring little regression to produce, which were formerly banned may suddenly become acceptable and poetic.

Given these considerations, we should expect metaphor distance to increase with movement from cell 1 through cells 2 and 3 to cell 4 of Figure 3.1. At a high level of elaboration, deep regression should be expected to produce images of greater metaphor distance than shallow regression. But a movement to low elaboration and shallow regression should produce even further increments in metaphor distance. Finally, deep regression and low elaboration would produce maximal metaphor distance. Thus we see that style, content, and metaphor distance are all interrelated. The poet cannot produce images of a given degree of metaphor distance *in vacuo*; rather, to obtain such an image he must regress to a certain depth and then elaborate the product of this regression at a specific stylistic level. More or less regression or elaboration would produce an image of other than the requisite degree of metaphor distance. From another perspective, once we know the values of any two of these variables, we should be able to predict the value of the third.

THE EFFECT OF POETRY

Metaphor Distance and Arousal

Any communication is intended to or tends to reinstate in the receiver the state of consciousness of the sender. The effect of poetry, then, ought to be the same as its cause: alteration in level of physiological arousal and concomitant regression. There is indeed evidence that art in general has such effects. The pioneering work of Berlyne (1960, 1967) has shown that the collative aspects of stimuli (novelty, incongruity, surprisingness, complexity) are major determinants of arousal. Berlyne (1971) holds that such stimulus qualities are also central to art. His (Berlyne, 1960) early work has shown that the collative aspects of stimuli have reward value, that both animals and humans, rather than seeking drive reduction and a state of quiescence, in many situations actually prefer and seek out novel, complex, and surprising stimuli. Presumably, this is because such stimuli increase arousal, which within a certain range is felt as pleasurable. Berlyne (1967) hypothesizes that pleasure and the arousal potential of a stimulus are related as shown in Figure 3.2. Medium increases in arousal are experienced as pleasurable, while larger increases induce displeasure. Smaller increases are of neutral hedonic value. A similar approach is taken by McClelland et al. (1953), who hypothesize that "positive affect is the result of smaller discrepancies of a sensory or perceptual event from the adaptation level of the organism; negative affect is the result of larger discrepancies."

Other aspects of stimuli besides their collative properties influence level of arousal. Most important are what Berlyne (1971) terms *ecological properties* (meaningfulness) and *psychophysical properties* (intensity, size, pitch, and so on). Schneirla (1959) and Berlyne (1967) have reviewed studies which support the idea of an

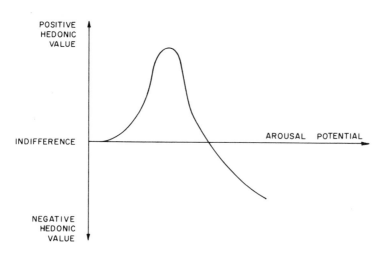

FIGURE 3.2 Hedonic tone and arousal potential (after Berlyne, 1971, p. 89).

inverted-U relationship between arousal and hedonic tone, so a few examples will suffice at this point. Such relationships have been found by Lehmann (1892) and Haber (1958) for judgments of pleasantness of water temperature and by Engel (1928) and Pfaffman (1960) for taste preferences as a function of concentrations of various substances. Turning to aesthetic stimuli, inverted-U relationships have been demonstrated between pleasingness and size of polygons by Martin (1906) and between pleasingness and both intensity and pitch of tones by Vitz (1972). Similar relationships between preference and complexity have been reported by Day (1967) and Vitz (1966) for visual stimuli, by Evans (1969) for prose passages, and by Kamman (1966) for poetry. Berlyne (1971) discusses further findings which suggest similar results for other collative properties such as novelty, surprisingness, and incongruity.

In light of these considerations, it would seem that such terms as *beauty*, *quality*, *goodness*, and *greatness* refer to poetry characterized by medium levels of metaphor distance. These terms refer to what is *liked* by the poetic audience, especially the audience of critics. Thus, beauty follows the same curve in relation to metaphor distance that liking does to arousal potential in Berlyne's formulation. Since metaphor distance is systematically related to both poetic style and content, our prediction concerning it has implications for these variables as well. The poet must avoid both extreme banality and extreme novelty. In so doing, he will be confined to poetry exhibiting intermediate levels of regressive content and intermediate levels of stylistic elaboration.

Now other factors influence arousal besides the characteristics of the particular stimulus being focused upon. Berlyne (1971) lists normal diurnal variations, high drive states (e.g., hunger, fear, anxiety, sexual arousal), and intellectual or muscular effort as variables which increase arousal. Of course, "background" stimulation would also contribute to a person's level of arousal. As might be expected, high levels of arousal seem to lead to decreased preference for novelty, complexity, and so on. McReynolds (1958) and Zuckerman, Kolin, Price, and Zoob (1964) found that anxiety decreases preference for novelty. Berlyne and Crozier (1971) allowed subjects to look at either a simple or a complex design. More preference for the complex design was found when the prestimulation environment was dark than when it was enriched. Analogous findings with rats are reported by Berlyne, Koenig, and Hirota (1966). On the other hand, sensory deprivation has been found to increase preference for complex, unpredictable stimuli (Jones, Wilkinson, and Braden, 1961). These experiments deal with momentary increases or decreases in arousal. There is some reason to believe that chronic high arousal states may lead to a movement of the curve depicted in Figure 3.2 to the right; that is, to the establishment of an adaptation level which requires *more* complexity or novelty to induce pleasure. Berlyne (1971) suggests such an explanation for the consistent finding (Fischer, 1961; Kavolis, 1968; Lomax, 1968) that more complex art is preferred and produced in complex societies than in primitive societies. The complex type of society involves more information input on a number of levels, and this leads to the establishment of a higher arousal baseline. Stimuli having complexity sufficient to induce moderate increases in arousal from this baseline will necessarily be more complex than those sufficient to induce moderate increases from the primitive's lower baseline. On another level, creative subjects have consistently been found to prefer more complex, novel, and surprising stimuli than uncreative subjects (Barron and Welsh, 1952; Houston and Mednick, 1963). The results of five studies examining basal EEG activity have indicated a fairly consistent tendency for creative subjects to exhibit slightly higher levels of cortical arousal, as measured by absence of EEG alpha waves, than uncreative subjects (Martindale, 1974b). It would seem reasonable to tie the differences in preference for novelty to this physiological difference.

Preference for a work of art should be a function of that work's arousal potential and the perceiver's level of arousal. Arousal potential is a function primarily of collative characteristics (metaphor distance in the case of poetry) but also of psychophysical characteristics (e.g., size, intensity, and so on) and of ecological characteristics (e.g., meaningfulness and drive incentive features such as sexual explicitness). The perceiver's level of arousal is a function of the arousal potential of "background" stimulation and, perhaps, of long-term physiological individual differences. Since more creative subjects and, by inference, artists prefer greater novelty than less creative subjects, who could be seen as composing the average expected audience for poetry, poems of relatively low metaphor distance which would be acceptable to the audience are too banal for the artists; on the other hand, those of relatively high metaphor distance which would be acceptable to the poets are unacceptable to the audience. In the next chapter we shall work out the consequences of this disequilibrium for literary change and add a third determinant to our preference equation.

Metaphor Distance, Regression, and
the Function of Art

If we were right in holding that states of consciousness are based on level of arousal, then showing that art leads to a change in the latter shows, *ipso facto*, that it induces an altered state of consciousness. Such regression need not be extreme. Ever since Aristotle's catharsis theory, the arousal of emotion has been given an important part in art. Even the most didactically oriented and secondary-process oriented theories of poetry (e.g., Johnson or Pope) see the arousal of emotion as important in getting the poet's message across. Schachter (1959) has produced evidence to uphold his contention that emotion consists of a state of physiological arousal and a cognitive label. On a more general level, Fischer (1971) argues that the characteristics of altered states of consciousness in general may be seen as joint functions of subcortical arousal and cortical interpretations of this arousal. Thus art may be of use in practicing the experience and labeling of emotions and states of consciousness.

The individual automatically attempts to apprehend or understand any stimulus presented to him. In Goldstein's (1939) terms this consists of making oneself "adequate" to the stimulus, coming to terms with it, responding adequately to it. Poems exhibiting extreme metaphor distance are ambiguous, incongruous, illogical, and impossible or unrealistic in varying degrees. To the degree that they are so, they cannot be dealt with by means of the usual secondary process mechanisms of understanding. However, they are perfectly amenable to apprehension by primary process systems of logic. The idea of projective testing in psychology and of the silence of the analyst in psychoanalysis is, by presenting an ambiguous situation or stimulus, to strip away the rational, reality-oriented modes of coping with the world and to lay bare deeper levels of consciousness and personality. The same function is served by contemplation of insoluble riddles, or *koans*, in Zen Buddhism and of the doctrine of the trinity or the immaculate conception in Christianity. Bateson et al. (1956) have stressed the importance in the etiology of schizophrenia, which is a type of pathological regression, of mothers who continually put their children in "double binds" by communications which carry contradictory messages on different levels. The poet, then, puts the reader into the same sort of double bind as does the Zen master or the schizophrenogenic mother and, like them, induces regression.

Modern aesthetic theory holds, however, that art has the potential for more than the induction of voyages into "inner space." If we believe with Sokolov (1963) that the brain is, at base, essentially a device for the analysis of novelty and incongruity, then art is seen to be of central importance, since it is so rich in these variables. Peckham (1965) hypothesizes that the social function of art is to provide a setting for what in our terms would be controlled regression in order to provide exercise for the audience in both handling and producing unexpected stimuli.

Chapter 4
A PSYCHOLOGICAL THEORY OF LITERARY CHANGE

Make it new.
POUND

INTRODUCTION

The Sociological Matrix

In regard to the social context within which poetry is produced, we may isolate a poetic subculture or system that consists on one level of orienting values, norms concerning the production of poetry, and a set of roles. The role of poet articulates the creative personality with the poetic subculture in two ways. First, it recruits into the system individuals who will be able to perform the poetic function. This function is served by a sort of resonance with the personality types who will be able to create poetry. When maximally efficient it should also operate to turn away individuals who would be unable to create poetry. Second, it must shape the recruited personalities so that their creative potential is actualized. This is done by articulation with the various norms governing the production of poetry.

Both roles and norms actualize the orienting values of the system. We understand these values to be the guiding beliefs of the system such as those concerning the social function of poetry and the various implicit rules which determine what poetry is. These values exert a cybernetic control over norms and roles, which may change in order to facilitate the fulfilling of values. Presumably, if we were able to determine the highest values governing the poetic system we should be able to explain the static and dynamic attributes of the norms, roles, and products of the system. However, since such values are temporally quite stable, it would seem unlikely that change in the product could be due merely to change in the orienting values.

Determination of values is not a simple matter of examining poets' theories of poetry. We must assume with Mannheim (1936) that a social system tends to generate a certain ideology that rationalizes and legitimates its operation, a "theory" that may be somehow isomorphic to truth but is not exactly true. Changes in the theory of poetry, just as changes in the role of poet and norms governing its production, are part of what is to be explained by a theory of literary change. They cannot themselves be taken as explanations. Poetry does not change because the theory of poetry changes; rather, both change together in the service of some less obvious cause.

There is also the level of social organizations, which may be construed with an economic analogue: the poetic product is exchanged with some audience in return for either money or intangible rewards such as deference or fame. Mediating this exchange may be various systems of distribution (e.g., publishers, libraries, booksellers) and critical organizations (e.g., literary critics).

Control of the Creative Product

We have a plethora of possible influences on the creative product. On the organizational level both the audience and the interchange mechanisms can exert influence and control. Clearly, poetry must be influenced by the orienting values of the poetic system, yet just as clearly it must be conditioned by its psychological means of production. But these potential influences differ fundamentally in character. The poet may anticipate the desires of the audience or of critics but the latter cannot influence the poetic product in a direct way, else they would end by writing it themselves. Clashes with the values of the larger society may silence certain poetic themes, but can they create others? Are we not dealing here, as with the intrapsychic processes by which poetry is elaborated, with hierarchic controls which can modulate and delete but cannot create of themselves?

Sorokin (1957), in formulating his *principle of immanent change*, has spoken to this problem:

> As soon as a sociocultural system emerges, its essential and "normal" course of existence, the forms, the phases, the activities of its life career or destiny are determined mainly by the system itself, by its potential nature and the totality of its properties. The totality of the external circumstances is relevant, but mainly in the way of retarding or accelerating the unfolding of the immanent destiny; weakening or reinforcing some of the traits of the system; hindering or facilitating a realization of the immanent potentialities of the system; finally, in catastrophic changes, destroying the system; but these external circumstances cannot force the system to manifest what it potentially does not have; to become what it immanently cannot become; to do what it immanently is incapable of doing. Likewise, the external conditions can crush the system or terminate an unfolding of its immanent destiny at one of the earliest phases of its development (its immanent life career), depriving it of a realization of its complete life career; but they cannot fundamentally change the character and the quality of each phase of the development; nor can they, in many cases, reverse or fundamentally change the sequence of the phases of the immanent destiny of the system. (Sorokin, 1957, p. 639)

How is one to determine the degree to which the system is autonomous and unhindered? Sorokin specifies several factors: the degree of integration or cohesion of the system and its power. What are the senses in which the poetic system may be autonomous in relation to its audience and to higher-level extrasystemic values? First, in regard to the audience, there are several variables which should facilitate autonomy:

1. Integration of the poetic system as opposed to the integration of the audience: Here we understand the relative cohesiveness, sharing of values, and potentials for interaction of the two systems.

2. Power: By power we mean not only physical or political power, of which poetic systems tend to have little, but also "rational" power or status derived from fulfilling higher values of the society.

3. Control of mechanisms of distribution: Here the question is whether the poetic subculture has control over critical and distributional organizations or whether these are differentiated and independent systems.

4. Dependence upon interchange with audience: To what extent is the poet dependent upon the monetary and other returns from the audience for fulfillment of his basic needs? In modern

times, this comes down to the empirical question of whether the potential audience is large or powerful enough to offer even the possibility of supporting the poet, whether potential demand warrants the cost of distribution of the product.

In regard to extra-artistic value systems, several other factors are important in determining autonomy:

5. Social function of poetry: If this is clearly defined, the audience can manipulate it against the poet. If poetry serves a liturgical purpose, it cannot be profane; if everyone agrees that its purpose is entertainment, it cannot be boring. To the extent that the social function of poetry is ambiguous, a putative social function cannot be very effective in determining its course.

6. Personal alienation of the poet: To the extent that alienated individuals have been recruited, the poetic system will be less easily moved by calls to higher-level social values.

To the degree that the poetic system is autonomous, in the ways listed, to that degree the system itself controls the poetic product. Let us consider what implications for literary change arise from different degrees of autonomy.

IDEAL CASE OF COMPLETE AUTONOMY

Sociological Considerations

A completely autonomous poetic system is no more possible than is a completely unautonomous one. However, the autonomous system is of great theoretical significance. In this case, we imagine that the attributes of autonomy outlined here are maximal. Where now, though, may we seek the causes of literary change? If the poetic system is completely autonomous, we have a condition with no inputs either from the larger society or from specific audiences. Given this, must we not, in the general case, imagine an inertia in all aspects of the system? Indeed we may but, retaining the physical analogy of Chapter 1, we remember that in a vacuum, moving objects continue to move indefinitely: entropy derives from environmental friction (i.e., from the audience). When biological organisms are placed in "vacuums," where survival is easy, there may be a similar inertia: paleontologists have discovered mastodons whose curving tusks had continued their course through the skull and into the brain; sabre-toothed tigers apparently became extinct because their incisors grew to such exacerbated lengths as to prevent eating. As will be seen, these are apt analogies for the course of modern poetry. Let us return to Sorokin:

> As long as it exists and functions, any sociocultural system incessantly generates consequences which are not the results of the external factors to the system, but the consequences of the existence of the system and of its activities. As such, they must be imputed to it, regardless of whether they are good or bad, desirable or not, intended or not by the system. One of the specific forms of this immanent generation of consequences is an incessant change of the system itself, due to its existence and activity. (Sorokin, 1957, p. 639)

This passage holds the key to the problem of why art changes. On one level, the answer is a sort of purloined letter: it has to change. The most basic thing about the artist is that he creates; but to create means to bring into being something *new* or, at the very least, something different. Originality is relative to what has come before; by its working, the creating of original responses, the artistic system changes the meaning of what is original. Even the mere constraint that the artist produce objects which are different would eventually lead to a cumulation whereby later products were less likely, more original, than earlier ones.

Now if the poet did not have to produce different and original products, one could become a great poet merely by copying out great poems; we should make no differentiation between the typesetter and the poet. The differentiation between creator and reproducer is the first to emerge historically; before this differentiation we are dealing with bards, magicians, and priests. If we imagine any of the latter in a completely autonomous system, we do not expect any originality constraint, but they are not poets or artists per se; as soon as one thinks of himself in any sense as an artist, he must value originality above reproduction.

Creation usually involves a good deal more than mere originality. It involves, perhaps, beauty and, certainly, some sort of usefulness criterion. But, considering the case of complete autonomy, creativity reduces to originality. Factors such as beauty and usefulness refer to the elaborational rather than to the inspirational process, and elaboration is directed toward communication. With complete autonomy, however, there is no communication. Is not a poet with absolutely no audience impossible? As attested by numerous poets, the audience or critic is internalized: "The classicist," observed Valéry, "is one who writes with a critic at his elbow." Of course, the romantic writer merely moves the critic back; he cannot remove him altogether. Kris (1952) connects this prospective consciousness of an audience with the process of elaboration: removing the audience is the equivalent of removing the reflexive nature of the poet's consciousness. It leaves a poet who produces but does not examine and hence does not elaborate or give coherence to his productions, a poet with no interest in communication, a poet with regressive inspiration but no secondary elaboration. Complete autonomy thus implies "decorticate" poets, who do not elaborate but merely produce chaotic heaps of words.

The implicit need for originality is reinforced on other levels. It would seem that those recruited as poets tend to value novelty and to have an aversion to the commonplace. Alienation, another characteristic of the modern artist, implies a similar evaluation of novelty (cf. Durkheim, 1897). Empirically, the autonomy of a poetic system tends to covary with relative evaluation of novelty, and the need for novelty tends always to be the only unviolated law in such systems; it is much more stable than values on beauty and communication or rules concerning appropriate content, forms, or even syntax.

There are many examples of the importance of this constraint for originality. Pound's (1934) dictum, "make it new," expresses it succinctly. Giles (1923, p. 145) quotes the first rule in an ancient T'ang book on the poetic art as follows:

> Discard commonplace form; discard commonplace ideas; discard commonplace phrasing; discard commonplace words; discard commonplace rhymes.

Hugo, in a letter to Baudelaire,[1] commented,

> I have never said: art for art's sake; I have always said: art for the sake of progress. . . . What are you doing when you write those striking poems. . . . You are advancing. You are endowing the sky of art with some macabre ray. You create a new thrill.

Baudelaire himself put it as follows:

> We wish, so much this fire burns our brains,
> To plunge to the depths of the abyss, Hell or Heaven,
>   what does it matter?
> To the depths of the Unknown to find something new!
>   *Baudelaire,* "Le Voyage"

[1] Quoted by Shroder (1961, p. 77).

The importance of novelty for literary change has been noted before. There is the perhaps apocryphal story of the undergraduate who demonstrated the point by sending some of Shakespeare's lesser-known sonnets to various literary reviews, only to have all of them rejected. Rosenberg (1959) has emphasized this "tradition of the new" as it appears in explicit form in modern art. This constant pressure for novelty leads, according to the considerations of the last two chapters, not to a prediction of random variation or of increasing chaos but to predictions of a quite specific nature which order an only apparent chaos.

We have hypothesized that the basic value in an autonomous artistic system must be originality. This leads to actions by the system that, in accordance with the principles set forth by Sorokin, change the system. Thus the problem of how the system and its products can change without change in values is illuminated. But what precisely changes in the product? One may seek originality on the level of content or form, but the central variable of the poetic product is its metaphor distance, the probability of co-occurrence of its elements. This must change if the value on originality is to be met. Norms and roles in the poetic system must change in order to facilitate fulfillment of the value on originality. It is the psychological principles governing the production of original responses that condition all of these changes.

Associationistic Formulation

The initial inspiration for the present theory was derived from the observation that Mednick's (1958, 1963) models of schizophrenia and of creativity are similar and that the former even more than the latter could be applied to literary history. Mednick, working within an associationistic framework, likened the creative process to a word association task: around all words are associative gradients based upon the probability that a specific word will be given as a response to the stimulus word in question (i.e., based upon the strength of the S-R link between the words). The less the probability of a word occurring as a response, the more original its emission is. Mednick hypothesized that highly creative individuals have flatter associative gradients than do uncreative individuals. That is, in creative people, common associates (e.g., chair-table) are less strongly bonded than they are in less creative subjects; the reverse is true of uncommon associates (e.g., chair-ocean). Creative and uncreative individuals have essentially the same networks of associations. Presented with the word *table* both will give similar initial responses. However, the creative person is able to continue associating while the uncreative person ceases to respond. The creative individual has a more extensive network of associates and the strength of the bonds is spread out more evenly.

Mednick's model of schizophrenia also starts from an associationistic perspective. In this case he reasoned that schizophrenic verbalizations and thinking are bizarre (and, thus, original) because of avoidance gradients around key words and themes; in thinking about them, the schizophrenic avoids common associates and emits remote ones, thereby avoiding the anxiety that has become conditioned to the stimulus words. As anxiety becomes more severe, the strength of these avoidance gradients increases, and the individual's thought and speech become increasingly bizarre and incomprehensible.

Now, this model can be applied to the poet: If he must always create more original responses than have preceding poets, then for him too there are avoidance gradients (which expand over time) around key words and themes (see Figure 4.1). Given a finite number of possible poetic subjects, later similes and metaphors *must* join more remote associates than earlier ones if they are to

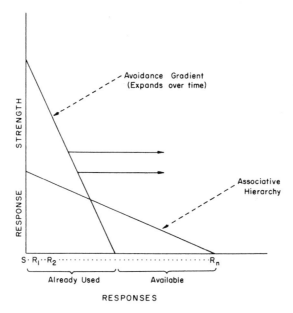

FIGURE 4.1 Associative model of literary production.

be adjudged acceptable. Where Shakespeare says of the moon that she is "an arrant thief and her pale fire she snatches from the sun," Musset in his "Ballade à la lune" compares the moon shining over a steeple with the dot over an *i*. Both of these comparisons make sense, though Musset's strikes us as more remote and strange. A more radical shift is seen in the movement from, for example, Swinburne's "mother and lover of men, the sea" to Breton's "seas red like the egg when it is green."

If this model is correct, there must, over any length of time, occur a sort of "schizophrenization" of poetry. In other words, given the limiting conditions in regard to autonomy from the larger society, literary history is isomorphic to coming down with schizophrenia. This view has affinities with Werner's (1948) argument that the origin of metaphor lies in primitive taboos on the utterance of certain words. In modern times, it appears that the "taboos" continue to generalize without limit in the case of the creative artist. This application of an associative theory of creativity to literary history provides us with a good model of the course of metaphor distance over time and leads us to expect certain parallels between the course of sections of literary history and the course of schizophrenia, but it does not specify anything about the psychological processes used to achieve this expansion. It seems clear, however, that Mednick's theory of originality may be joined with the regression theory of inspiration in that regression entails more free-associative thinking or, in other words, a loosening of associative bonds and a flattening of associative hierarchies. Osgood (1957) similarly derives originality from flat associative gradients and points out that, according to Hullian theory, either very high or very low levels of arousal should produce such a flattening. The associative theory of creativity and the regressive theory that we have espoused may, then, be seen as emphasizing different psychological aspects of the same physiological *Anlage*.

Regression Formulation

The creative product is a joint product of cognitive regression or dedifferentiation and subsequent secondary elaboration. This view was articulated with the concept of metaphor distance in Chapter 3; the postulated relationships were diagrammed in Figure 3.1. Original similes can be produced using either close or distant associates, but with a high level of elaboration, some potential similes (e.g., "A table is like a chair") are rejected as nonsensical and therefore uncreative. No such distinction is made at lower levels of elaboration. We recall this model only to collapse it. Complete autonomy must be seen as removing not only the external audience but the internal one as well; there can be no secondary elaboration but only production of the raw material of regressive inspiration. In terms of Figure 3.1, this leads to the collapsing of the two-dimensional structure into a straight line representing the continuum from slight regression and strong associative bonding to deep regression and weak bonding with concomitant free-associative thought. Metaphor distance would in this case move, in the service of increasing originality, from cells 1/3 to cells 2/4 in Figure 3.1. Obviously this comes down to the case arrived at by extrapolation from Mednick's associative model. In the present framework we are able to say that, in a completely autonomous system:

1. Metaphor distance will increase in such a way that it is completely reducible to the average strength of associative bonds between poetic stimulus words and the responses with which they are paired to form similes. If poets in such a system were to produce similes concerning the word *table* we would expect the following series based upon Russell and Jenkins' (1954) word association norms: "A table is like a chair," "A table is like food," "A table is like a desk," "A table is like a top," "A table is like a leg," etc.

2. There will be continually increasing regression by the poet. The content of poetry should change so as to reflect the deeper and deeper levels at which it was produced. If the system were made autonomous at a hypothetical point of minimal metaphor distance, content should at first contain secondary process words and then progress through levels of emotion, sensation, drives, and finally, to oral oceanic and narcissistic indicators. In short, we should expect changes in content to be in accordance with the multiple criteria of regression summarized in Chapter 2.

3. Poetic form should show continual disintegration. In terms of the ranges of style defined in Chapter 3, if the system were made autonomous at a point of minimal metaphor distance, poetic form should disintegrate from discursive, through analogical and equational, to juxtapositional style.

Thus, in a vacuum, poetry would be predicted to move away from the classical and rational through deeper and deeper levels of regression until it reached some hypothetical point beyond which regression and metaphor distance could not be pushed. At that point poetry should cease to exist. Now, in relative terms, such a point was reached around the end of the last century, the point beyond which mystics cannot "bring back" their discoveries, at which Rimbaud and Valéry gave up poetry in disgust. Poetry did not vanish, however, but continued by different means. Style and rules were changed to allow poetry to continue to be written. The problem with the ideal case of complete autonomy is that we are unable to explain abrupt stylistic changes. By eliminating ego and audience we also eliminated the structural aspect of poetry and, with it, the possibility of stylistic shifts. The model of poetic production in a state of complete autonomy may approximate changes in *content* for short periods of time in cases where, as in modern times, the set of poets and the set of readers are virtually identical. However, we must bring in the audience if we are to explain the stylistic or structural shifts that have kept poetry from becoming a burned-out art.

MIXED CASES

Audience Pressures

In line with our belief that poetry is conditioned most basically by intrasystemic factors, let us begin with the ideal case where autonomy is infinite and gradually reduce the autonomy of the poetic system. With the first increment we replace the reflexive nature of the poet's consciousness, and with successive ones we replace his audience and articulation with the larger society. If the originality constraint is the analogue of gravity, the audience exerts a frictional or retarding influence.

As Grosse (1893) observed, "Nearly every great work of art is created not conformably to, but against, the prevailing taste. Nearly every great artist is not chosen but rejected by the public." It is a commonplace that the history of poetry could be chronicled around the highly predictable critical attacks on each new school of poetry. Squarely at the center of such attacks is often secondary process revulsion against the "illogicality" and "absurdity" of the productions of these new schools. One has only to read Nordau's (1895) work to see the very real rage which poetic ambiguity and novelty can produce. The same thing is seen in a different form in Johnson's far more secure righteous indignation throughout his *Lives*. As an example, take his comments on the absurdity of the first stanza of Gray's "Progress of Poetry."

> Gray seems in his rapture to confound the images of "spreading sound and running water." A "stream of musick" may be allowed; but where does "musick", however "smooth and strong" after having visited the "verdant vales, rowl down the steep amain" so as that "rocks and nodding groves rebellow to the roar?" If this be said of Musick, it is nonsense; if it be said of Water, it is nothing to the purpose. (Johnson, 1779-1781, Vol. 4, p. 469)

In juxtaposing and merging sound and water, Gray expands metaphor distance beyond the point which Johnson deems acceptable; it is unacceptable precisely by virtue of its commission of the twin faults of any rational framework: it is meaningless and it is irrelevant. Similarly, a contemporary critic in a review of Keats' "Endymion," a review where *unintelligible* appears in practically every paragraph, said of Keats,

> he is unhappily a disciple of the new school of what has somewhere been called Cockney poetry, which may be defined to consist of the most incongruous ideas in the most uncouth language. (Croher, 1818)

Flatter (1948) has shown how, on a more insidious level, successive editors of Shakespeare have eliminated irregularities in meter and verse and made them more and more regular.

In light of these observations, it is perhaps surprising that a pressure for novelty, indeed, seems to operate on the audience as well as on the poet. We have seen in the last chapter that any poetic audience, unless it is specially selected, will dislike ambiguity *more* than will those in the poetic subculture. Then, to the extent that an audience has power (in the sense of patronage or necessity for sales) over a poet, we may expect that the poet will be restrained from excessive ambiguity or metaphor distance. Of course, almost any audience goes to art in search of a *moderate* degree of ambiguity and regression.

In Chapter 3 we argued that preference for a work of art is a function of the arousal potential of the work and the perceiver's level of arousal. This is strictly true only for the initial exposure of a work. We must take familiarity into account, since arousal potential generally habituates or decreases with repeated exposure. Experiments in which aesthetic stimuli are repeatedly shown to subjects and judgments elicited or looking time observed may be taken as experimental analogues of art history. The time scale, of course, differs, but the principles governing the two situations should be comparable.

Several studies have assessed the effect of repetition of the same stimulus. Berlyne and Parham (1968) repeatedly presented subjects with colored polygons and asked for ratings of novelty after varying numbers of presentations. Judged novelty declined as a function of number of presentations. Using the same paradigm, Berlyne (1970) found similar decreases in rated pleasingness and interestingness as a function of number of presentations. Skaife (1967) found that liking for popular music decreased with repeated presentations while Alpert (1953) and Skaife (1967) found increases in preference for more complex music, with repeated presentations. Using repeated presentations of paintings, Berlyne (1970) found decreasing preference for simple and increasing preference for complex stimuli. Repetitive presentations of the same painting, as opposed to presentations with other paintings interspersed, led to quicker decreases in liking for simple paintings and to decreases rather than increases even for complex paintings.

Research involving successive novel presentations as opposed to successive presentations of the same stimulus have been less clearcut. While decreases in exploration time (Day, 1966; Haywood, 1962; Leckart, 1967) and physiological responsiveness (Berlyne et al., 1963; Kratin, 1959) have been found, Berlyne and Parham (1968) found slight increases in rated novelty. Greater preference for novelty and complexity are found in those with more aesthetic experience than in those with less (Munsinger and Kessen, 1964), which may be interpreted as more previous extraexperimental trials with successive novel stimuli. Finally, subjects given choices between successive recurring versus successive novel series of stimuli shift their preference to the novel series (Berlyne, 1958; Leckart, Briggs, and Kirk, 1968). In such situations, subjects prefer slight as opposed to extreme discrepancies from the recurring stimulus (Connors, 1964).

Several extrapolations are possible from this body of research. Even in very low-autonomy artistic traditions and even where artists value imitation of old models rather than originality, we can expect some pressure for change. This might even arise from the audience rather than the artist: given that some pleasure is expected from art, and that repetition leads to decreasing pleasure, an intrinsic pressure toward change for the purposes of maintaining the level of this pleasure should exist. The longer a given style has existed, the greater should this pressure for change be. Further, the results of Berlyne (1970) suggest that pressure for change should be greater where the artistic product is simpler and where the audience is exposed more unremittingly to it. Pressure for novelty arising from the audience should be greatest in simple art forms to which the audience is constantly exposed (e.g., popular music). Given the curvilinear relationship between complexity and pleasingness and the research results concerning increases in liking for complex art as a result of number of exposures, we should expect the audience to resist change in the more complex arts.

Finally, these experiments suggest that changes in preference should be gradual, toward slightly new art rather than toward radically different products. The results of one aspect of Berlyne and Parham's (1968) experiment even cast light on why shifts in preference often seem to be toward revival of old styles. Subjects viewed eight consecutive presentations of one stimulus, one presentation of one of a different color and shape, four more presentations of the initial stimulus, and then a second presentation of the other stimulus. Rated novelty decreased over the first eight presentations and increased markedly for the new stimulus, as would be expected. However, when the old stimulus was shown again, rated novelty was slightly higher than on its last presentation but resumed its decline. Finally, the second presentation of the other stimulus was rated more novel than the preceding stimuli but lower than on its first appearance. In its serial context, even something seen before may be subjectively felt as novel.

Even if artists did not generally feel a pressure for novelty arising from their role, we see that the audience would force change upon them. The reason for emphasizing intrinsic rather than extrinsic pressures is that intrinsic pressures seem to be empirically more important in initiating literary change. Further, since artists theoretically prefer more novelty and resist extreme novelty less than the audience, extrinsic pressure is more important in retarding the search for novelty than in advancing it. It is clear enough, though, that if no audience *ever* accepted a work, we would not ordinarily even think of it as belonging to literary history. Thus, the retarding effect of the audience is not absolute but temporary and relative.

To those familiar with the approach–avoidance model upon which our extrapolations from Mednick's theory were based, it will be obvious that to Figure 4.1 we can add an avoidance gradient generated by the audience (see Figure 4.2). The steepness and extent of this second avoidance gradient depend upon the power of the audience over the poet and, of course, the audience's attitude toward novelty. Where the audience's power is great and its intolerance of ambiguity is also high, the gradient will extend farther toward the left, thus disallowing a large number of possible

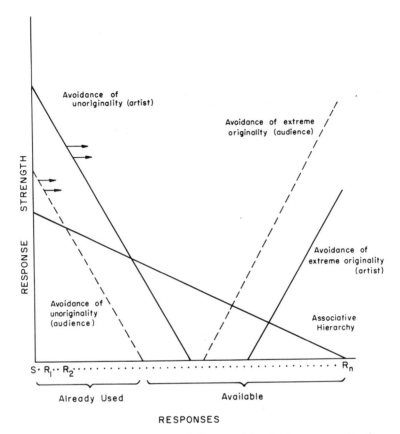

FIGURE 4.2 Expanded associative model of literary production, showing avoidance gradients due to pressure to avoid extreme originality (*right*) and unoriginality (*left*).

metaphors. This is the position of much eighteenth-century poetry. As well, it must be noted that, given the neoclassic character of the times, the gradient governing avoidance of already-used types of images was weaker. This conspired toward an unoriginal bias in the poetry of the age. In general, artists would also be expected to avoid extreme novelty and the audience to avoid extreme lack of novelty. However, as may be seen in Figure 4.2, these latter gradients may be ignored since they fall within ranges already ruled out by the gradients just described.

In the audience's avoidance of originality, ambiguity, and regression, there is a greater pressure against absurdity than against obscurity; there is a greater pressure to maintain adequate elaboration than to avoid regressive content; there is a greater preference for juxtapositions that, however distant, belong to logically similar categories than for juxtapositions that make less sense logically although they may exist in a context of shallow regression. Coming down to the level of poetry per se, there is a greater resistance toward changing its structural or stylistic aspects than toward changing its content. This is because of the differential arousal potentials of the two factors.

Basic Formulation

We expect a poetic tradition to maintain a given style until its regressive potentialities are exhausted rather than to exhibit a series of stylistic shifts with regression maintained at a constant level. There must come a point, however, at which the system can better tolerate some sort of stylistic disintegration rather than further increases in regressive content. This point will be determined by the power of the audience over the poetic subculture and the bias of the audience toward secondary process cognition. At such a point, there should be a shift toward less regression and less elaboration such that the *net* level of regression minus elaboration is not appreciably changed but there is possibility of (1) an unbroken continuance of the expansion of metaphor distance and (2) another regressive cycle on a new level. Figure 4.3 illustrates this shift for two cases of differing degrees of

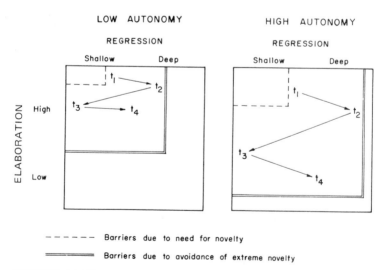

FIGURE 4.3　Predicted changes in regression and elaboration for two degrees of autonomy for four successive points in time (t_i).

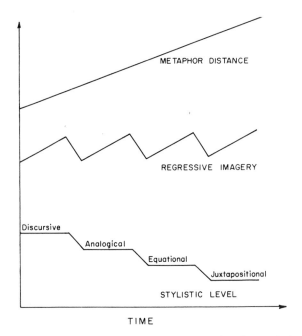

FIGURE 4.4 Predicted changes in the theoretical parameters as a function of time in an autonomous system.

autonomy. Figure 4.4 gives an illustration of the hypothesized course of metaphor distance, stylistic level, and regression as a function of time. With lower autonomy, regression is allowed to proceed less far and stylistic shifts are less far-reaching. Of course, with low autonomy, events in the larger society would be expected to impinge more upon the poetry, thus further obscuring the trends. Both of these cases, of course, assume a sufficient valuation of originality to support the continued expansion of metaphor distance. Where originality ceases to be so valued a classical reaction toward less metaphor distance and regression might well be expected. Empirically, however, such reactions seem usually to be mediated by decreases in autonomy.

Let us review briefly the major implications of the theory for mixed cases ("medium" degrees of autonomy):

1. Metaphor distance increases continuously. The rate of increase of metaphor distance is a function of the autonomy of the system: the more autonomous, the steeper the rate of increase.

2. Within any given style, regressive imagery (as manifested in the content of poetry) increases because poets are forced to

regress more and more in order to achieve the requisite degree of metaphor distance.

3. Periodically, there should be periods of stylistic change. During these, stylistic level should "disintegrate" to less-elaborated levels: i.e., from discursive to analogical to equational to juxtapositional. These stylistic changes allow regression to decrease while permitting further increases in metaphor distance.

4. The role of poet should change so as to recruit those who would be able to create poetry of the requisite degree of metaphor distance. This generally means that those with potentials for greater and greater degrees of regression should be recruited; the personality types recruited should approximate more and more closely the model of the originality-producing personality described in Martindale (1972b).

5. Poets' theories of poetry should change so as to describe and rationalize the changes occurring in the system. Thus, after a certain point, beauty and communication of universal human emotions would not be likely contents of such theories.

6. Finally, as a corollary exercise, were literary critics to comment upon the changes in content, role, theory, etc., it should be possible to "translate" their descriptions into the terms of the psychological theory.

We have argued that preference for a given work of art is a curvilinear function of the work's arousal potential and the perceiver's basal arousal. There is some reason to believe that the perceiver's basal arousal may be divided into at least two components. Chronic, or long-term, arousal seems to be positively related to preference for metaphor distance, complexity, etc., at least within a medium range. On the other hand, momentary increases in arousal seem to be negatively related to such preferences. Given this, it would follow that chronically high arousal states in the artistic subculture and/or audience should lead to rapid rates of artistic change while momentary high arousal states should retard such change. Berlyne's (1971) hypothesis that social complexity is accompanied by higher arousal states is consistent with the apparently more rapid rates of change in most complex societies. Other factors that might be expected to produce chronic high arousal states would be sustained rapid social change, urban environment, and high levels of social mobility. Even climate (cf. Taine, 1863) could have an effect. Heat may be seen as inducing arousal (Provins, 1966). Given the inverted-U relationship between chronic basal arousal and artistic preference, we might predict that the art of temperate societies should exhibit higher rates of change than the art of tropical or arctic societies. Zajonc (1965) argues that mere presence of other people increases arousal. Thus, variables such as population density and, indirectly, social solidarity or cohesiveness should influence the rate of artistic change. Rapid momentary increases in arousal could result from wars, depressions, and revolutions; such events should retard artistic change.

The arousal potential of a work of art is a positive function of its psychophysical, ecological, and collative properties and a negative function of its time-in-series, or how often it or similar works have been repeated. Metaphor distance and its analogues are one type of collative property. Rate of change in metaphor distance must be influenced by the other factors determining arousal potential. Works having a high arousal potential by virtue of their psychophysical characteristics ought to be less likely to exhibit high levels of metaphor distance or high rates of change in the latter because these in combination with the psychophysical properties would push arousal potential too high and result in negative hedonic tone. For example, more incongruity, novelty, and surprise, and faster rates of change in these variables should be found in small than in large works and in works employing weak rather than intense stimuli. Other things being equal, the design of large public buildings should change more slowly than that of smaller private residences. Perhaps music tends to change more slowly than the other arts since, as compared to silent reading of a poem, say, it is more intense. Within the field of music we ought to expect rate of change to be a negative function of intensity (works for string quartets should change more quickly than orchestral works or operas) and pitch (music for the flute should change less quickly than piano music).

On the level of ecological characteristics, works depicting contents of high meaningfulness should change slowly and exhibit low levels of incongruity. For the believer, sacred art possesses high arousal potential because of its significance; added arousal due to change or incongruity would push affect into the negative range. On another level, paintings of nudes induce some degree of sexual arousal and thus leave less room for variation in collative properties. Thus nude painting should change slowly. Finally, "abstract" painting, having little or no intrinsic meaningfulness, ought to change rapidly.

We have tended to lump most collative characteristics such as novelty, incongruity, and surprisingness under the rubric of *metaphor distance*. But these are rather clearly distinct from complexity. From our arguments here, it follows that simple arts should change more quickly than complex ones. Such relatively simple arts as popular music and clothing do seem to change extremely rapidly. This is somewhat obscured by the weak "memory" of the system in which they are produced, so that cycles and oscillations, rather than longer, unbroken evolutionary sequences, result. Other things being equal, arts already exhibiting extreme levels of metaphor distance should change in smaller and smaller increments.

Finally, familiarity and repetition effects must be reckoned with. Arts consumed by audiences that spend a good deal of time with them should change more rapidly than those supported by occasional consumers. On the level of the utilitarian arts, we would expect everyday eating utensils to change more rapidly than silverware reserved for special occasions, sitting room furniture to change more rapidly than bedroom furniture, casual clothing to change more rapidly than formal wear, and so on.

REFINEMENTS

We have taken one aspect of the poetic situation and worked out its consequences. By no stretch of the imagination should the theory be construed as explaining all changes in poetry, even in any of the periods of maximum relevancy. What is claimed is that such dynamics are more important in explaining these changes than is usually thought, that they do indeed explain many of the basic changes in certain artistic series. However, a number of provisos, caveats, and additions are needed to round out the theory.

"Entelechy" versus "Natural Selection"

Schücking's (1923) and others' treatments of the audience of art have shown that one cannot speak of the audience in general terms. There are many different types of audience which operate according to quite different laws. A similar treatment of such terms as *the artist* and *modern poetry* is needed. As often used, such terms have no more meaning than *the younger generation* or *modern man*. This is because they are sampled in a consistently and cumulatively biased manner. It is not uncommon to see chains of reasoning wherein "the modern condition," say, is inferred from the condition of the modern artist, which is inferred from the condition of the most eminent modern artists, which is in turn inferred from these artists' "representative" (i.e., best or most unique) productions.

Before worrying about sampling, however, some consideration must be given to the population. Here, clearly, is a case of many being called and few being chosen. The series of authors constituting literary history is generally taken to be the few successful writers rather than the mass of "attempted" ones. We have framed our theory largely in terms of "attempted" writers, in terms of an inner push toward novelty; but similar dynamics were shown to operate in the critical audience. The difference is usually that the audience experiences a lesser aversion to the old and a lesser attraction to the new than do the writers. As autonomy increases, the artist moves faster than the critical audience and especially than the lay audience; but, since originality is relative, the audience does move. This is why even very regressive or high-metaphor-distance poets eventually gain access to the ranks of the chosen; as long as we do not approach too closely to present-day poets, it is not a serious distortion to test the theory using "chosen" rather than "attempted" poets as the population.

Reverberatory Circuits

In anything as complex as the history of an art form, one cannot expect unidirectional causality. Perhaps the most important relevant example is the vicious circle set up beyond a certain level of autonomy. Autonomy heightens the value placed upon novelty, leading to increases in metaphor distance (and to concomitant increases in regression or stylistic disintegration); but these changes make poetry less palatable to the audience and thus lead to further increments in autonomy, which feed back into an even greater valuation of novelty, and so on. Beyond a certain threshold, the processes we have described ought to speed up in a geometric fashion, with quicker and quicker successions of stylistic disintegration. This can be termed *stylistic slippage*. As autonomy approaches its maximal level, stylistic disintegration should tend to become continual rather than occurring in noticeable periodic leaps.

On another level, the things we have taken as rationalizations have an effect of their own. If a given poetic manifesto rationalizes current practice, it also exerts some causal effect on future practice. Those observers who trace changes in poetry to changes in poets' theories of poetry are not altogether wrong. Our contention has been merely that it is more profitable to invert the conventional perspective.

Residual Traits

The personalities recruited to fill the role of poet carry with them a number of traits not needed by the role. These may be idiosyncratic or general. An example of a general trait is connected with the tendency of the role of poet to draw alienated and unconventional individuals (since they tend to produce original responses) given to more rebelliousness than is the general population. This may lead to a tendency toward revolt and iconoclasm for their own sakes. Many see such rebellion as basic to stylistic change. A new generation may change a given practice merely because previous generations have performed it in a certain way. While one cannot deny that such gratuitous change may occur, placing it at the center of one's theory leads to unfruitful dualistic thinking. Thus, the Parnassians obviously revolted against the emotionality of their romantic predecessors. Implicit dualistic assumptions have led perhaps most commentators to see this as a reaction back toward classicism. While the poets of this generation did talk a good deal about form and style, the content of their poetry (see Chapters 5 and 10) makes it clear that, on a more basic level, they continue the regressive voyage upon which the romantics set out.

On another level, let us examine an example of a residual role trait. Sartre (1950) and Graña (1964), among others, have provided a great deal of evidence that the role of poet in France after 1800 is patterned on the eighteenth-century role of the aristocrat. This was functional, since the aristocrat provided a nonutilitarian image congruent with the regressive aspects of the creative personality. Particularly in the earlier years of the century, the role offered the possibility of projecting the poet's hatred of secondary process cognition onto the secondary process oriented activities of the bourgeoisie. But the aristocratic *Anlage* had certain fairly autonomous consequences. Certainly it provided a sort of security not felt by, say, American poets. Beyond this, it maintained the autonomy of the poetic subculture for almost a century by closing off any interest in an establishment of alliances with proletarian antibourgeois political movements. Had this aristocratic image not been present, poets might have heeded the call of the Saint-Simonians to establish a didactic, utilitarian art.

The aristocratic nucleus further tended to draw only a certain segment of regressive personalities; in nineteenth-century French poetry there is a certain apotheosis of inhumanity and cynicism (aristocratic disdain for the masses often served as a code for hatred of humanity in general) such that Fowlie (1967) aptly subsumed aspects of it under the title *Climate of Violence.* The subjects studied by Maslow (1962), who are in some senses also regressive personalities, show that this attitude is not common to all such types. The connection between regression and religion suggests the same conclusion.

As long as values other than originality are in effect, they too generate effects of their own much as does the originality constraint. Values on beauty, entertainment, or communication have consequences not wholly reducible to the originality value. We argue that these are lower-level values and are discarded when their fulfillment hinders meeting the originality constraint. It would be foolish to argue that, before they are discarded, they have no effect.

External Conditions

As autonomy decreases, the portion of changes attributed to internal dynamics must decrease. On the level of current events, external factors may act by affecting autonomy; beyond their influence on level of arousal, wars and revolutions may increase the valence of stimuli connected with the external society and thus lead to a functional reduction of autonomy. Wars, for example, seem often to exert a push toward solidarity which is not unfelt by the poet. The role of former surrealists in the French Resistance during World War II is a case in point. On the other hand, social stress tends to produce novel stimuli which catch the poet's attention regardless of his feelings of social solidarity. For example, the writings of Baudelaire and Flaubert on the disorders of 1848 make it quite clear that, while they regarded the aims of the rioters as monstrous, they were overjoyed that something interesting was happening.

On another level, the density of potential poets (and of a potentially sympathetic audience) in the larger society cannot but have an effect upon the poetic subculture. This density can be attributed to a number of factors which are obviously extrapoetic. Changed values and changed child-rearing practices can indirectly affect the poetic subculture. For example, the tendency for artistic periods of flowering to follow periods of upheaval may be due to such factors as father-absence in such periods, which leads to increments in the number of potential poets (cf. Martindale, 1972a). Some social factors may have a more or less direct effect upon poetic autonomy. Authoritarian political regimes may take direct measures to snuff out artistic autonomy, whereas permissive regimes may take no such action. Escarpit (1958) provides some interesting empirical evidence concerning the effect of authoritarian political regimes on the recruitment of poets and writers.

CONTEXTS OF APPLICATION

The basic fact about modern poetry is that it has no audience to speak of. Auden put is as follows:

> The ideal audience the poet imagines consists of the beautiful who go to bed with him, the powerful who invite him to dinner and tell him secrets of state, and his fellow-poets. The actual audience he gets consists of myopic schoolteachers, pimply young men who eat in cafeterias, and his fellow-poets. This means that, in fact, he writes for his fellow-poets. (Auden, 1948, p. 176)

The autonomy of modern (post-1800) poets is based largely upon two related factors. First, poetry has no clear social function: the novel and the theater usurped poetry's last remaining function—that of entertainment. Second, the poetic audience is very small. Even if he pleased the potential audience fully, the serious poet could not make a very good living. Commentators (e.g., Poggioli, 1968; Schücking, 1923) are agreed that the readership of contemporary poetry after 1800 has been miniscule. Further, the poet's audience has changed radically. Schücking (1923) shows that before the late eighteenth century, the audience consisted largely of members of one class with homogeneous values and opportunities for face-to-face interaction. Organization of the audience was high and, with patronage, it exerted effective control over the artist. After this time, the poetic audience was self-selected from a number of classes with different values. Members of the audience had no opportunities for interaction, usually did not even know who other members were, and were not numerous enough to exert economic control. Beyond these factors, the poet, regardless of his rather ambiguous social status in the eyes of the larger society, has very high status in the eyes of what extrapoetic audience does exist. Valéry's remark to Mallarmé that there was one young man in each city in France willing to give his life for Mallarmé sums up the condition of the poet: he has an almost astronomically high status in the eyes of a very small, disorganized, and powerless following. These factors are such as to lead to a great deal of autonomy. Further, the poetic subculture has taken up the functions of distribution and consumption as well as production. The system of interchanges between poet and audience has dedifferentiated so that poets tend to print "little magazines" and distribute them among themselves. There is relatively little leakage to the larger society. The romantic poets were confronted with a distinct body of extra-poetic critics. As late as the 1850's Baudelaire remarked that it was an impossibility for a critic to become a poet, thus underlining the differentiation of the roles. The Pre-Raphaelite Brotherhood marks a sort of turning point: the tendency of members to review each other's works led to outcries concerning a conspiracy of critic and artist. But the outrage became the practice; Valéry and Eliot are clear examples of the merging of roles of artist and critic.

The above considerations apply to most poetry written after the late eighteenth century. However, there are clear differences in autonomy. French poetry is universally conceded to have been in the vanguard of change since around 1850. Several factors conspired to make French poetry more autonomous than English and other poetry. The French poetic subculture has exhibited considerably more organization and power than the English. The status of the artist in France is high in a less ambiguous fashion than it is in England. This is due to a number of reasons: the long association of art with the French aristocracy, the tendency for French artists to "usurp" the role of aristocrat, and the relatively lower general valuation in France of utilitarian, achievement-oriented activities. In regard to cohesiveness, French poets have tended to form close-knit schools and movements with clearcut organizations; these usually have a clear leader and clear status hierarchies, and issue manifestoes, etc. In England, on the other hand, poetic organization is much lower. The reason for this is probably extrapoetic, having to do with what might be called the "English duke syndrome"—in England there seems to be tendency for high-status individuals not to interact with peers but with distinctly lower-status individuals; the English have no rules or inclinations for the making of minute discriminations in status which are necessary if dukes or poets are to interact in an organized system. The French (cf. Versailles under Louis XIV) are, on the other hand, adept at this. These differences may condition the difference in poetic organization.

The theory is, then, maximally relevant to French poetry after 1800 since this poetry exhibits maximal autonomy. Interestingly, French culture works against the predictions of increasing unconscious dominance and chaos. As Gide has said, "In France and in France alone, intelligence always tends to win over emotion and instinct." French culture prizes consciousness, rationality, moderation, order, and clarity (cf. Hazard, 1940; McClelland, 1963; Metraux et al., 1950); French poetry came, after 1800, to move away from all of these values.

The course of English metaphysical poetry is also maximally susceptable to explanation by the theory. The poetry of this school was written almost exclusively by amateurs (who supported themselves by their extraliterary professions) to be handed around within their select circle in manuscript form, was almost never published in contemporary periodicals, and was totally ignored by contemporary critics. While the poets were not alienated on the level of personality, the poetic system was almost completely insulated from any external audience.

Any differentiated poetic system possesses more autonomy than might commonly be thought. It is shown in Chapters 8–14 that even English eighteenth-century poetry, a system with comparatively low autonomy, follows a course predicted by the theory. Systems which seem to possess low autonomy often do not. This is clear in painting, where autonomy often arises from high status rather than from lack of an organized audience. The high prices Picasso received for his paintings tell us that he had high status, not that his audience had the potential to exert control over him. Similar considerations apply to nineteenth-century academic art. Reitlinger's (1961) study of the price movements of paintings makes it evident that, correcting for currency devaluations, the "worst" academicians such as Alma-Tadema or Bougeureau received prices analogous to those received by eminent painters today. In addition, such painters' membership in academies increased organization. Sixteenth-century mannerist art constitutes another case of autonomy deriving mainly from high status rather than from lack of interchange with the audience.

It must be emphasized that the theory does not imply, e.g., that metaphor distance has increased linearly over all time or that all poetry is characterized by continual cycles of increasing and decreasing regression. The theory applies only where its initial conditions are met. Perhaps most important, it applies only to sets or series of poets who constitute in some sense a system. For example, it would not be predicted that twentieth-century

American poetry exhibits higher metaphor distance than seventeenth-century French poetry. Except in a very vague sense, modern American poets do not see the seventeenth-century poets as their predecessors; they therefore feel no constraint to surpass them. Even in more related systems metaphor distance may decrease over time. Eighteenth-century English poetry almost certainly exhibits much lower metaphor distance than does seventeenth-century English metaphysical poetry. The two systems do not really form a continuous series. The metaphysicals wrote in a sort of autonomous "poetic pocket." The situation of eighteenth-century poetry was one of less autonomy in general. Many poets of that time either were not familiar with metaphysical poetry or, with Johnson, rejected it as unpoetic, as something to be forgotten rather than surpassed.

SUBSUMPTION OF DESCRIPTIVE "LAWS"

One test of a theory's power is its ability to subsume the postulates of less general theories. In Chapters 5 and 6 we shall have occasion to reinterpret or derive a number of statements by literary critics, but here we are concerned with deriving from the theory several more general descriptive laws. Praz (1933) cites extensive evidence to support his contention that nineteenth-century European literature describes a *parabola of the sexes*. Where, at the beginning of the century, males were described as strong and females as weak, over the course of the century these roles were gradually reversed. Where the beginning years of the century are dominated by the Byronic hero, by Promethean and Satanic figures, its closing years saw the figure of the persecuted, enslaved, and androgynous male come to the fore. Concomitantly, the persecuted maiden gave way to the femme fatale: the figure of Salome in, e.g., the works of Flaubert, Wilde, Mallarmé, and Swinburne became dominant. Praz supports his generalization with a large number of examples. In Chapter 12 we present statistical evidence, based upon a content analysis of nineteenth-century French poetry, which decisively upholds the generalization.

The pattern recalls in reverse the course of archetypal development in both the individual and the race as described by Jung (1959) and Neumann (1954). The same pattern occurs in the alchemical experiment (Jung, 1944, 1956): opposite elements, symbolized as male and female principles, are first purified and isolated in exacerbated form and then melded together to form a more perfect substance symbolized as an androgyne. The patterns are the same because the psychological laws underlying both processes are the same. In Chapter 10 we provide quantitative support for the theoretical prediction that French poetry was, from 1800 to 1900, written at deeper and deeper levels of regression. Over time, poets capable of and inclined toward successively deeper levels of regression were recruited in the service of the search for novelty. Given this, we can predict Praz' "law." Even if one rejects Jung's idea that the different images of the sexes symbolize different stages or levels of regression, the prediction would follow from the model of the creative personality developed in Martindale (1972b): those capable of deeper regression may be more likely than others to have a life history in which the mother is dominant and the father absent or passive and thus to view sexual roles in the predicted fashions.

Shroder (1961) uses the analogy of the flight of Icarus to describe the changes in the role of the artist in the nineteenth century. During the first half of the century, he contends, the role of poet was flamboyant, active, assertive, and heroic (e.g., Hugo, Balzac), while in the last part of the century such aspirations were largely given over, and the image of the artist came to emphasize impotence, withdrawal, and passivity (e.g., Flaubert, Mallarmé). Where Praz deals with poetic content, Shroder deals with the role of poet, but both reach analogous conclusions. Shroder's descriptive law can also be derived from the theory. If it was necessary to recruit poets given to and capable of ever deeper regression, it would be necessary to recruit those who were more given to passivity, who were blocked from action, who sought adventure in reverie rather than in the world or even in fantasy.

Ortega y Gasset (1948) has described changes in literature over this same period of time as exhibiting a fundamental "dehumanization." Reality has been increasingly deformed; its human aspect, its meaning, has been destroyed. In regard to the objects depicted, there has been a reversal: formerly trivial objects came to the fore in place of important or meaningful ones. Emotion and pathos have been banned. Artists have increasingly sought to divest art of its functions, increasingly come to say that it has no transcending significance or meaning, that it is merely a form of gratuitous play. Where "before reality was overlaid with metaphors by way of ornament; now the tendency is to eliminate the extrapoetic, or real, prop and to 'realize' the metaphor, to make it the *res poetica*" (Ortega y Gasset, 1948, p. 34). Similarly, there has been an increasing focus on ideas per se as opposed to the things the ideas represent, implying a withdrawal from reality into fantasy.

All of these generalizations can be deduced from the hypothesis that poetry was written at increasingly deeper levels of regression over the course of the nineteenth century. Contents which have emotional, human meaning are well worked over by the secondary process. With regression, there is a decreasing tendency to differentiate figure from ground, to divide objects into significant and insignificant. Like the acute schizophrenic, the poet is oversensitive to stimuli but undersensitive to their abstract meanings. In a very real sense, he has lost interest in the world; the Virgin, the king of France, became merely stimulus patterns on the order of a potato or a blade of grass. On the psychological level, this can only mean that regressive thought processes have come to the fore. Similar considerations apply to the artist's insistence that art is useless and meaningless. Dress designers can usually offer extensive commentaries on the meaning and relevance of what they are doing, but great poets often give flippant answers or say they have no idea. They do not know or cannot say because their products make sense only on a regressive level. The meaning cannot be translated back into a form that makes sense on the secondary process level. Baudelaire and Mallarmé seriously defined poetry as sorcery; it makes sense to see such definitions as referring to the regressive nature of the states of consciousness from whence their poetry flowed.

Ortega y Gasset's last generalizations are quite important: metaphor has changed from ornament to the central core of poetry, and the focus of poetry has changed from things to "ideas." In Chapter 5, we shall see that the French poet started out by trying to think of metaphors or similes to describe his ideas or perceptions and ended with the production of metaphors by the quasirandom collision of words on a free-associative level. At first, poetic analogy was purposive: one sought similes in order to describe how he felt or what he saw. Similes described real objects. This has not at the highest levels of poetry been true for over 150 years. Gradually, "objects" came to be *created* by collisions of words which produced new, unreal and impossible objects. Poetry ceased to *refer* to anything at all and came to be, in Breton's words, "pure psychic automatism." It was not ideas per se which came to be central but words, which came more and more to be apprehended concretely. All this is what would be expected from production at deepening levels of regression: thought becomes free-associative and ceases to refer to real objects; words come to be apprehended as things.

SIMILAR THEORIES

A number of thinkers have presented theories which are in one way or another similar to the one presented here. These constitute independent convergences from a number of different starting points and within a number of discrete theoretical frameworks. Peckham (1965) employs perceptual and expectancy theory (e.g., Bruner et al., 1956) on the psychological level and some of the tenents of symbolic interactionism with an emphasis upon communication (e.g., Mead, 1934) on the sociological. He concentrates upon the audience and its responses where we have concentrated upon the poet and his methods of production. For somewhat different reasons both theories postulate that the effect of art upon its audience is regression (although Peckham does not use the term), that the eliciting vehicle is incongruity, and that incongruity is the central variable to be considered in any artistic product. Peckham concentrates upon incongruity or disruption of expectation on the formal level (his term is *discontinuity*) while we have concentrated on it on a more contentual level (metaphor distance). Both theories also find expansion of metaphor distance/ discontinuity to be basic to the very nature of the artistic enterprise and tie the rate of expansion to social factors. Peckham emphasizes the amount of time or energy the audience devotes to art, while we have stressed the autonomy of the artistic sub-culture. Peckham seems to assume a purposeful fabrication on the part of the artist where we have seen such fabrication only as a sort of second thought after the original regressive inspiration. Because of this initial assumption, no changes in the process of creation are seen as necessary to produce increasing numbers of discontinuities. Peckham's theory thus cannot explain changes in the content of art which accompany changes in the level of discontinuity, nor can it explain changes in the role of artist or the recruitment of artists. Meyer (1956) has developed a theory of change in music which is similar in many ways to Peckham's general theory. The major problem with such formulations is that, as we argued in this chapter, the audience lags behind the poet, especially as autonomy increases; given this, there are difficulties in ascribing changes primarily to the audience.

The present theory is perhaps closest to one developed by Maritain (1953). The latter deals with post-Renaissance art, but most specifically with poetry. Both theories say that, especially after the eighteenth century, poetry has been written at increasingly regressed levels. Maritain traces this back to the splitting off of the theater and the novel from poetry, which left poetry free to pursue its basic function: intuitive apprehension of "transreality" and self-knowledge. Maritain develops a model of regressive thought in which a "musical unconscious" is differentiated from the Freudian unconscious. This "musical unconscious" yields intuitive knowledge, in the pursuit of which poetry follows its regressive course. A good many modern poets have said that their poetry constitutes a sort of arcane knowledge, but Maritain may be accepting rationalizations rather than realities when he takes them at their word. At any rate, it is not possible to specify what this knowledge is or even what exactly it is knowledge of. Where, for example, we see the discarding of rules over the course of time as being in the service of the achievement of greater originality, Maritain (1953, p. 221) sees it as being in the service of a closer approximation to "the soundless music stirred by poetic intuition within the soul." Both theories agree that modern changes in poetry are due to its being divested of secondary functions; there is disagreement concerning the primary function which remains and concerning the nature of the regression to which this primary function leads.

Kahler (1968) has described breakdowns in the form and coherence of the arts since the late eighteenth century in terms of increasing dominance of the unconscious mind. This is analogous to increasingly more regressive origins of art over this era. Kahler postulates a straightforward and continuing regression over this period until very recently when (e.g., with the "behavioristic" *nouveau roman* school of Robbe-Grillet and Sarraute) there has been a revulsion away from the "depths." This process is tied to factors in the larger society and in the history of ideas: for example, the cycle began with "a weariness of rational discipline among the ruling nobility and intelligentsia" in the eighteenth century (Kahler, 1968, p. 73). Kahler's model of regression is not well enough developed to account for what might be called the central fact of modern art history: the stylistic change around 1900 where content becomes *less* regressive while form becomes more regressive.

Perception of the outer world involves a number of built-in corrections. One sees a distant figure of a man as larger than a nearer figure of a child although the size of the latter on the retina is larger. Similarly, a white object in shadow and a black object in bright sunlight may actually exhibit the same shade of gray, but unless the context is cut off from view they are seen as being distinctly different colors. We see what we "know" is there, not what the actual sensations depict. These corrections, or constancies, were first scientifically investigated by the nineteenth-century psychophysicists, who were, however, very much struck with the fact that painters had, over the course of time, discovered and utilized these constancies. Ehrenzweig (1953) investigates this artistic discovery of constancies and argues that the sequence of discoveries can be laid at the door of constantly increasing delibidinalization of the external world by artists and consequently increasing dominance of their work by what we would call regressive thinking.

From the Renaissance until around 1900 painters increasingly painted not perceptions but sensations. The Renaissance saw the development of perspective, which can be equated with a loss of form constancy: artists began to paint objects not the size they are but the size they appear to be on the retina. In the baroque era the invention of chiaroscuro techniques involved the violation of brightness, or local tone, constancy. With the impressionists, constancy of color is violated: one no longer painted objects their "true" color but the color they appeared to be. One might conclude, with Riegl, that the cause of this was a desire to depict reality more adequately. Ehrenzweig, on the contrary, argues that it was due to increasing detachment, to a loss of interest in the world with a consequent weakening of the "surface mind" or secondary process (the organ of apprehension of the outer world). This in turn led to a lack of interest in external things; along with this went the artist's lack of interest in what he painted: it increasingly made no difference whether it was the Virgin Mary or a potato.

The course of art after impressionism supports Ehrenzweig's contention, for the process of disruption continues beyond a point where the audience can reintegrate what is painted. According to Ehrenzweig, Cézanne made the crucial step in this process. Cézanne violates certain constancies of peripheral vision so that the tendency to integrate a large number of momentary fixations into a total gestalt is lost. Cubism is seen in this framework as a violation of constancy of localization: cubist objects are often depicted from two angles which could not be seen simultaneously. With abstract expressionism, there is a complete disintegration of the "thing facade."

Ehrenzweig, as indicated, ascribes this progression to delibidinalization of the external world and concomitant unconscious dominance. He provides evidence that the constancies have been violated precisely in the order of their importance to the conscious, or surface, mind. One can consciously abrogate form constancy, but it becomes increasingly difficult to do so with brightness, color, peripheral vision, and localization. Ehrenzweig goes to rather extreme lengths to explain the artist's increasing loss of interest in the world. He ascribes this loss of interest to an eruption of irrational oral guilt in the Renaissance from unspecified and presumably unknowable sources in the unconscious mind. Ehrenzweig seeks to explain why the distortions of constancy were resisted by audiences when they were initiated but were taken for granted by later audiences with speculations concerning Lamarckian evolution. This is perhaps the best example of why a psychological theory of artistic change must be couched in a sociological framework rather than attempting to get by on a purely psychological level.

Why, one may ask, should the present theory be accepted over any of these others? The answer lies at two extremes of the criteria usually imposed upon theories. The theory is more comprehensive than Peckham's: it can explain changes in poetic content more fully than can his theory. At the other extreme, it is more parsimonious, precise, and falsifiable than those of Maritain, Kahler, and Ehrenzweig. We assume an explicit psychology where Maritain's is almost mystical; where Kahler reaches to the highest levels of general culture for explanations we need go no further than the artistic subculture; Ehrenzweig relies upon Lamarckian speculation where we rely upon explicit sociological assumptions. On another level, and most important, the present theory is constructed so as to lead to testable predictions, and has indeed been submitted to systematic empirical testing.

Part II
QUALITATIVE EVIDENCE

Chapter 5
MODERN FRENCH POETRY

> *Of all of the influences active in the history*
> *of literature, the chief is the influence*
> *of work on work.*
>
> BRUNETIERE

We have argued that there is a sort of tragic flaw involved in the production of poetry. Like Malthus' theory of population, our theory derives certain unavoidable consequences from inexorable conditions in the structure of a situation. Poets must strive to be more original than their predecessors. We have examined the implications of this constraint in light of the psychological means for the production of poetry. In this, a sort of psychic Marxism was espoused, and, appropriately enough, yielded predictions analogous to those of Hegel (1835) concerning the "interiorization of Spirit." We have compared the course of modern French poetry with an alchemical experiment and with the development of schizophrenia; on a less metaphorical level, we have argued that it involved recruitment of poets given to increasing depths of regression, who produced texts exhibiting greater and greater densities of regressive imagery.

In this chapter we shall attempt to provide evidence for these theoretical contentions. For each successive school of French poetry we shall discuss the theory of poetry, the role of poet, and the form and content of the poetry produced. Finally, we will look at examples that show the characteristic metaphor distance of the period. It would take hundreds of pages to do well what we have set out to do, but neither time nor space allows this. Given these constraints, it is impossible to provide even one example for every point made and difficult to avoid the impression of overgeneralization. But hundreds or even thousands of examples are not conclusive anyway; this is the rationale for the content analytic study reported in later chapters. The reason for this chapter must then be not so much to demonstrate as to give an idea of the data to be explained. A theory of schizophrenia would sound farfetched to one who had never seen a schizophrenic. Similarly, the theory presented in the last chapter may seem implausible if one is not familiar with any of the literary series to which it is most applicable.

CLASSIC VERSUS ROMANTIC

It is no novelty to point out that the dichotomy between classic and romantic parallels the dichotomy between secondary process and regressive cognition; as Gide has said, "The battle between classic and romantic takes place within every mind also." If this is true, then romanticism per se consitutes a shallow sort of regression. We will show that, after romanticism, there was a "romantic progression" toward ever deeper levels of regression, that finally, as Péret observed, "Dada was not a beginning but an end." Jones (1961) has described seven *axes of bias* on which he differentiates an *Enlightenment syndrome* from a *romantic syndrome*. We can easily identify the Enlightenment syndrome with eighteenth-century French cultural products and the romantic syndrome with French romanticism. A listing of the axes of bias shows that they refer to a secondary process versus primary process distinction:

1. Order versus *Disorder*: System, clarity, structure, analysis versus complexity, fluidity, disorder, novelty, chance, indeterminacy.
2. Static versus *Dynamic*: Calm versus change and frenzy.
3. Discreteness versus *Continuity*: Either-or division, pluralism versus unity, synthesis, inclusion, pantheism, monism.
4. Outer versus *Inner*: Objectivity versus experience.
5. Sharp-Focus versus *Soft-Focus*: Clarity, distinctness versus threshold phenomena, the ineffable.
6. This-World versus *Other-World*: The here-and-now versus spatial, temporal, or fantasy escape.
7. Spontaneity versus Process: Freedom, chance, accident, free will versus orderliness and lawfulness of things.

Romantic biases are italicized; according to Jones, there is no consistent difference on the last axis. It is fairly clear that these axes are not independent but that, on the psychological level, they reduce to secondary process versus primary process, with the romantic syndrome occupying the primary pole consistently.

ROMANTICISM

Theory of Poetry

French romanticism grew in some ways from Rousseau, the eighteenth-century cult of *sensibilité*, and such preromantics as Chénier; but it was also in large measure imported from English and German sources. Thus, it was in some ways more opaque and multidetermined than the later movements discussed. Romantic theories of poetry saw the poetic process as an expression of personality rather than as a representation of universal human truths. Inspiration and original genius were stressed. But the classical view of poetry as communication was retained: poetry has a role in educating the masses. In his preface to *Cromwell*, Hugo called for a loosening of poetic form and a synthesis of the beautiful and grotesque in a search for the sublime. Content was stressed over form; romantic poetry followed less rules and looser rules than did classical. Further, new content was allowed into poetry. The commonplace, the exotic, the humble, and the particular all became proper subjects for poetry as opposed to classical norms calling for only the exalted and noble, the universal and general. Such changes in stylistic rules suggest a lowering of the level of elaboration away from secondary process extremes. The call for a synthesis of the beautiful and the grotesque can be interpreted as a plea for greater metaphor distance: the two are disproportionate and unlike; therefore their union had been excluded from classical poetry.

Role of Poet

The "modal" romantic poet saw himself as superior, hypersensitive, and often cursed and persecuted because of his vision and genius. But he was given not so much to withdrawal as to action and adventure in the real world; he saw himself as a potential leader of men, a teacher and a prophet with a humanistic concern for the masses. The social self, or persona, was stressed, along with the megalomanic, Promethean identification of ego and ego-ideal. "Victor Hugo," said Cocteau, "was a madman who thought he was Victor Hugo." As for the poet being a leader of men, Chateaubriand and Lamartine both served in the foreign ministry of France, Hugo was deified in his later years as a national saint, Béranger was elected to parliament (but declined to serve), and Chateaubriand dreamed of finding the Northwest Passage. In later periods Mallarmé made a barely adequate high school teacher, Flaubert hardly ventured outside his house, and Baudelaire was incapable of handling his own finances. There was, to be sure, from the very first the image of the poet as passive and withdrawn, as exemplified by the *poètes poitrinaires*, but this type comes truly to the fore only in later years. Vigny, a transitional figure, spoke in his *Journal d'un poète*, of actively suppressing his "feminine," passive urges. This is important for many of the early romantic poets: Hugo and Chateaubriand often seem to have exhibited masculine protest against an underlying and latent feminine identification. Their early life histories suggest the possibility of such an identification due to father-absence and overcloseness to mothers and sisters.

Poetry

Romantic poetry is characterized by a number of themes: nature, sensations, emotions, the exotic in space and time, and sentimental and humanistic concerns. Nature replaced human interaction as the dominant focus. It was often apprehended in animistic, physiognomic terms; what Ruskin termed the *pathetic fallacy*—the attribution of emotion to inanimate objects—was rampant. Further, nature and external objects seem to have been used as screens onto which psychic regression was projected: ruins, night, and death often represented psychic disintegration. All nineteenth- and twentieth-century French poetry seems to represent at some level a quest for the Infinite. The romantics were able to find its emblems in finite, effable, at least conceivable forms: the vastness of the ocean, blue roses, the wildness of nature. For later poets, these finite manifestations of the Absolute were no longer satisfying, as will be seen.

Another important point is that French romantic poetry is discursive, rhetorical, and theatrical (i.e., aimed at the communication of a sentimental message) to the point that Hartley (1959) compares much of it to that low point of eighteenth-century English verse,

O Sophonisba, Sophonisba O!

One might even compare it to the satirical reply,

O Jemmy Thomson, Jemmy Thomson O!

Let us examine a specimen text which illustrates many of these romantic themes:

Thus, always pushed towards new shores,
Carried forever into eternal night,
Can we never on the ocean of the ages,
    Cast anchor a single day?
. . . .
O time, suspend your flight! and you, propitious hours,
    Suspend your course!
Let us relish the swift delights
    Of the most beautiful of our days!
. . . .
O lake! mute rocks! caves! dark forest!
You whom time spares or that it can rejuvenate,
Keep of that night, keep, beautiful nature,
    At least the memory!
. . . .
Let it be in your repose, let it be in your storms,
Beautiful lake, and in the sight of your laughing hills,
And in these black firs, and in these savage rocks
    Which hang over your waters!
                 Lamartine, "Le Lac"

Here we see many of the distinguishing marks of romantic poetry. There is concern with timelessness, but not timelessness per se (cf. "La Chambre double" below). There is some animistic or physiognomic perception but it is cast in a sentimental, apostrophizing, communication-oriented framework (cf. "Vers dorés" below). There are regressive themes but, as will be seen when the text is compared to later ones, they are modulated and suggest mild regression. The text stresses emotion, sensation, and nature as a projective device, and involves some animistic perception, but these exist in a context of rhetorical communication.

Metaphor Distance

An example from Chénier, a preromantic poet, gives us a sort of zero-point for metaphor distance:

Beneath your *fair* head, a *white delicate* neck
Inclines and would *outshine* the *brightness* of *snow.**
                Chénier, "Les Colombes"

*Italics added.

There is no metaphor distance to speak of; rather there is a consonant cumulation of connotatively similar qualifiers: only *delicate* and *brightness* contrast in even a slight degree. Romantic poetry extends metaphor distance beyond this point but in a form wherein the contrasts still make logical sense. The opening lines of Hugo's "L'Expiation" illustrate this:

> Waterloo! Waterloo! Waterloo! bleak plain!
> Like a wave which boils in an urn too full,
> In your arena of woods, of hills, of valleys,
> Pale death mingled the dark battalions.
>
> *Hugo,* "L'Expiation"

A plain and a sea, an urn and an arena are compared; this makes sense but the connotative overlap is not so complete as to be trite. In the last line, *pale* and *dark* contrast with each other if taken in isolation but do not clash insofar as their meaning in this context is concerned.

POSTROMANTICISM

Theory of Poetry

Gautier (1835), in his preface to *Mademoiselle de Maupin*, announced the doctrine of *l'art pour l'art*, or art for art's sake. Communication as a goal of art was renounced; the poem should be an object, not a message. Gautier, while retaining the romantics' orientation toward the exotic and toward sensation rather than cognition, rejected their sentimentalism, humanitarian concerns, and tendency toward rhetoric. He wanted to move wholly to the level of sensations. We may interpret this as a desire to move to greater depths of regression. The things he rejected—communication, human concern, even emotion—are secondary process phenomena. The Parnassians (e.g., Leconte de Lisle, Hérédia) followed him in the banishment of emotion and in the movement to the level of sensations.

Baudelaire opened the way for the even deeper regression of the symbolists. He spoke "of language and writing, taken as magical operations, evocatory sorcery" (Baudelaire, 1855-1862). The task of the poet, in this view, is to gain an arcane, mystical knowledge of the Beyond by deciphering the symbols offered in nature. In holding that the Infinite or the Absolute cannot be found *in* nature but *behind* nature, Baudelaire accepted a sort of

Swedenborgian mysticism. The method for gaining this mystical knowledge is synaesthetic perception, as is made clear in the sonnet:

> Nature is a temple where living pillars
> Sometimes let confused words escape;
> Man passes there through forests of symbols
> Which observe him with familiar gazes.
>
> Like long echoes which mingle far away
> Into a deep and dark unity,
> Vast like night and like light,
> Scents, colors, and sounds answer one another.
>
> There are some fragrances cool like the flesh of children,
> Sweet as oboes and green like meadows,
> —And others corrupt, rich, and triumphant,
>
> Having the expansion of infinite things,
> Like amber, musk, benzoin, and incense,
> Which sing the raptures of the mind and of the senses.
>
> *Baudelaire*, "Correspondances"

Thus, on the level of perception, Baudelaire called for a movement from animism to synaesthesia.

Role of Poet

Alfred de Vigny led in the transition of poet from actor in the world to actor in the depths of the self. He began his life with dreams of military glory but, cut off from this by the post-Napoleonic peace, he withdrew figuratively into his "tower of ivory," and literally to his manor house in the west of France. The poets of this period were no longer flamboyant prophets but passive seers. As Shroder (1961) contends, the distance between ego and ego-ideal was perceptibly widened. Flaubert and Baudelaire, the central literary figures of this period, exhibited a clear distaste, not for particular types of action or particular types of reality, but for action and reality as such. Where the romantics disliked the triviality of bourgeois life, Baudelaire hated the triviality of life itself. The exotic and the strange were no longer satisfying. For the romantics, the sea provided a symbol for the Infinite, but Baudelaire in "Le Voyage" spoke of "rocking our infinity on the finite sea." His tremendous need to escape the trivial, which was generalized to include the existent, is clear in the concluding lines:

> We wish, so much this fire burns our brains,
> To plunge to the depths of the abyss, Hell or Heaven,
>   what difference?
> To the depths of the Unknown to find something *new*.
>   Baudelaire, "Le Voyage"

In regard to the audience, it follows from the changes in the role
of poet and theory of poetry that the view was not sanguine.
There was little thought of communicating, let alone of leading or
enlightening. Poets were recruited who hated not one class but all
classes and all humanity.

Poetry

The verse of the Parnassians gives evidence of a source at a
deeper level of regression than romantic poetry:

> Noon, king of summers, spread out on the plain,
> Falls in sheets of silver from the heights of the blue sky.
> Everything is quiet. The air flames and burns breathlessly;
> Earth dozes in its dress of fire.
>
> The expanse is vast, the fields have no shade at all,
> And the spring where the flocks drank is dried up;
> The distant forest, whose edge is dark,
> Sleeps over there, motionlessly, in heavy repose.
>
> Only the great ripe cornfields, like a gilded sea,
> Roll into the distance disdaining sleep;
> As peaceful children of the sacred earth,
> Fearlessly they drain the sun's cup.
>
> Sometimes, like a sigh from their burning soul,
> From the bosom of the heavy ears which murmur among themselves,
> A majestic and slow undulation
> Awakens, and goes to die on the dusty horizon.
> . . . .
> Man, if, heart full of joy or of bitterness,
> Toward noon you passed into the radiant fields,
> Flee! nature is empty and the sun devours:
> Nothing is alive here, nothing is sad or joyous.
>   Leconte de Lisle, "Midi"

There is nothing in this poem except references to sensations
of a static, dreamy environment. When human emotion is
mentioned in the last stanza it is denied; metaphorically, the
audience is told to go away and mind its own business. In the last

line the romantic animism which Ruskin termed the *pathetic fallacy* is explicitly rejected. If we compare this passage with the selection from Lamartine, it is clear that the rhetoric, sentimentality, and secondary process contents have all disappeared.

It is also enlightening to compare the physiognomic perception evident in the selection from Lamartine with that in Nerval:

Man, free thinker! do you believe that only you think
In this world where life explodes in everything?
Your liberty disposes the forces that you have,
But the universe is absent from all your councils.

Respect in the beast an active spirit:
Every flower is a soul unfolded to Nature;
A mystery of love sleeps in metal;
"Everything is sentient!" And everything has power over your being.

Fear, in the blind wall, a gaze which watches you;
A word is connected even with matter . . .
Do not make it serve some impious purpose!

Often in the humble being lives a hidden God;
And, like an eye born covered by its lids,
A pure spirit grows beneath the rind of stones!

Nerval, "Vers dorés"

Where Lamartine's "laughing hillsides" strike us as deriving from relatively shallow regression, Nerval's eyes in walls and stones suggest inspiration at a deeper level. This is reasonable, since he was a schizophrenic. "Vers dorés" (along with Baudelaire's "Correspondances") forms the basis for French symbolism. It is not altogether unreasonable to suggest that Nerval's madness allowed him to anticipate the deeper regression of these later poets.

Baudelaire's prose poem "La Chambre double" illustrates many of the central themes of this era:

A room which resembles a reverie, a veritably *spiritual* room, where the stagnant atmosphere is lightly tinted with rose and blue.

The soul takes a bath of sloth there, flavored by regret and desire. —It is something twilight-like, bluish and rosy; a dream of delight during an eclipse.

The furniture has stretched out, prostrate, langourous forms. The furniture has the air of dreaming; one would say it was endowed with a sleep-walking life, like the vegetable and the mineral. The fabrics speak a mute language, like flowers, like skies, like setting suns. . . .

On this bed lies the Idol, the sovereign of dreams. But how is she here? Who brought her? What magic power installed her on this throne of reverie and of delight? What difference? She is there! I recognize her.

There indeed are those eyes whose flame penetrates the twilight: those subtle and terrible *optics*, that I recognize from their dreadful malice! They attract, they subjugate, they devour the gaze of the imprudent who contemplates them. I have often studied them, these black stars which command curiosity and admiration.

To what benevolent demon do I owe thus being encircled by mystery, by silence, by peace and by perfumes? O beatitude! what we generally call life, even in its happiest expansion, has nothing in common with this supreme life which I now know and that I savor minute by minute, second by second!

No! there are no more minutes, there are no more seconds! Time has disappeared; it is Eternity which reigns, an eternity of delights. . . .

Horror! I remember! I remember! Yes! this hovel, this dwelling of eternal tedium, is really mine. Here is the stupid, dusty, broken furniture: the fireplace without flame and without embers, dirtied with spit; the sad windows where the rain has traced furrows in the dust. . . .

Oh! Yes! Time has reappeared; Time reigns as sovereign now, and with the hideous old man has returned all his demonic cortege of Memories, of Regrets, of Spasms, of Fears, of Anguishes, of Nightmares, of Angers and of Neuroses.

I assure you that the seconds now are strongly and solemnly stressed, and each one, in spurting from the clock, says: "I am Life, unbearable, implacable Life!"

Baudelaire, "La Chambre double"

The poem chronicles a regressive vision followed by a return to reality. Regression is suggested by the strangeness of the room, the physiognomic quality of the furniture, and the explicit references to timelessness. In the regressive phase Baudelaire confronts an ambivalent "anima" figure. The disgust experienced upon return to reality and secondary process cognition is evident.

Baudelaire's regression has a sexual, lascivious tone that is lacking in later poets, but his sexuality is hardly of the mature, genital sort. His concern with filth and purity, the spiritual and the demonic, suggest an anal orientation. A clear example of this is his description of love making:

I advance to the attack, and I climb to the assault
Like a choir of worms after a cadaver.
    Baudelaire
    "Je t'adore a l'égal de la voûte nocturne"

Baudelaire's writings exhibit an ambivalence which has made it difficult for commentators to make much sense of him. In his journals he spoke of two simultaneous drives toward good and evil, angelic and demonic; and commented that it would be pleasant to be alternately executed and executioner. Perhaps this ambivalence stemmed from his tendency to think on regressed levels, where contradictions for logical thought cease to be contradictory.

Metaphor Distance

Some of these examples illustrate high metaphor distance, but it is interesting to quote the following verses from Baudelaire for comparison with the example from Chénier:

Her complexion is pale and warm; the dark enchantress
Holds her neck with a nobly affected air.
Baudelaire, "A une dame créole"

Where Chénier left us with no doubt about the color of the doves he was describing, we have no clear idea in this case: the woman is a creole, so we might expect her to be dark, but Baudelaire says that she is pale; once we have accepted this, he says that she is dark. One could argue about what he "really" meant but *uncertainty* is unquestionably higher than with Chénier's white white white white doves.

Another example from Baudelaire illustrates the juxtaposition of remote associates:

The violin quivers like an afflicted heart;
Melancholy waltz and languid vertigo!
. . . .
The sun is drowned in its clotted blood.
Baudelaire, "Harmonie du soir"

The following example from Gautier recalls certain metaphysical conceits:

And these pink folds [of a dress] are the lips
Of my unappeased desires,
Dressing the body from which you wean them
With a tunic of kisses.
Gautier, "A une robe rose"

Where the romantics tended to produce images composed of incongruous words made congruous by the sense or meaning, the postromantics moved toward more direct articulation of distant, but usually not completely incongruous, images.

SYMBOLISM AND DECADENCE

Theory of Poetry

The poets of this period avoided direct statements altogether in favor of indirect ones, with connotation being valued over denotation. The aim was to convey some sort of "knowledge" in this manner. Words were taken concretely and images formed not for the purpose of describing something but for the purpose of creating something. Images arose directly from free-associative combinations of words in states of deep revery rather than being composed in order to describe something experienced. The following quotations from Mallarmé's "Crise de vers"[1] illustrate these themes:

> Diction is too weak to express objects by touches corresponding to them in colour or in motion. . . . Beside *ombre*, which is opaque, *ténèbres* is not very dark; what a disappointment in face of the perversity that gives to *jour* and to *nuit* contradictorily, dark tones for the former and bright ones for the latter.

> The pure work implies the elocutory disappearance of the poet, who abandons the initiative to words mobilized by the shock of their inequality; they light one another up with mutual reflections like a virtual trail of fire upon precious stones, replacing the breathing perceptible in the old lyrical blast. . . .

> I say: a flower! and, out of the forgetfulness where my voice banishes any contour, inasmuch as it is something other than known calyxes, musically arises, an idea itself and fragrant, the one [flower] absent from all bouquets.

The first passage suggests that words are being apprehended concretely or at least connotatively; at the very least, they are not being used in a secondary process fashion. The second passage supports this belief and, further, suggests that the poet does not use words to describe or even to refer to anything; rather, the initiative is left to the words themselves as they collide with each other. The final passage refers to Mallarmé's belief in the incantatory or magical power of words and poetry, and it suggests that this absent flower, the "internal" one, is of interest.

Rimbaud's statement, "J'assiste à l'éclosion de ma pensée" ("I am present at the breaking forth of my thoughts") supports the contention that the images of this period were created by collisions of elements in free-associative states. If this is so, then the images no longer *refer* to anything; where the earlier poet sought words and images to describe his feelings or ideas, these poets were presented with images that, in a sense, created new feelings or ideas. Verlaine expresses some of the same ideas in a more straightforward fashion:

[1] Hartley, 1965, pp. 166, 171, 174.

Music before everything,
And for that prefer the Uneven
More vague and more soluble in the air
With nothing heavy or stationary in it.

Also you must not
Choose your words without some obscurity:
Nothing more dear than the grey song
Where the Vague joins with the Precise.

. . . .
For we still want the Nuance,
Not Colour, nothing but the nuance!
Oh, the nuance alone betroths
Dream to dream and flute to horn!

Flee as far as possible from the murderous Epigram,
Cruel Wit, and lewd Laughter
That make the eyes of the Azure weep
And all that common kitchen garlic!

Take eloquence and wring its neck!
Verlaine, "Art poétique"

Verlaine here calls for the rejection of secondary process aspects of poetry connected with communication—epigrams, wit, eloquence. Direct statement is banned; rather, the poet should choose his words on the basis of sound, music, and vague connotations. Obscure words are preferred since their multiple meanings give more opportunities for incongruous and ambiguous statements. The call for joining the vague and the precise similarly suggests an interest in increased incongruity.

This period also saw a degree of stylistic disintegration. In the late 1880's Kahn and Laforgue introduced free verse. Mallarmé, while he tended to retain old verse forms, often mangled and distorted syntax. Yet there tended not to be a massive disintegration of style such as occurred in the twentieth century. If these poets spoke of impossible things, they usually did so in a grammatical and understandable, if difficult, form.

Mallarmé exhibited a "phobia" against direct naming: to name the object was to destroy it. He wished "to paint not the thing, but the effect it produces."[2] We recall that in Mednick's theory of schizophrenia a similar process is postulated. Certain elements become anxiety arousing, and the schizophrenic therefore moves outward on the associative gradients surrounding these elements. Rather than thinking about a word directly, he thinks about its

[2] Quoted by Fowlie, 1953, p. 145.

remote associates. This causes thought to become confused and bizarre. A similar process seems to have been operant in the symbolists. Their "phobia" against denotative naming arose, of course, from the need for novelty based upon their position in the poetic series.

Role of Poet

As suggested by the quotations from Mallarmé, the poet assumed a passive role in this period. Rimbaud's "Lettre du Voyant"[3] provides a role prescription:

> For *I* is someone else. If brass wakes up a trumpet, it is not its fault. To me this is obvious: I witness the unfolding of my own thought: I watch it, I listen to it: I make a stroke of the bow: the symphony begins to stir in the depths, or springs on to the stage. . . .
> But the soul has to be made monstrous, that's the point. . . . Imagine a man planting and cultivating warts on his face.
> I say that one must be a *seer*, make oneself a *seer*.
> The poet makes himself a *seer* by a long, prodigious, and rational *disordering* of *all the senses*. Every form of love, of suffering, of madness; he searches himself, he consumes all the poisons in him and keeps only their quintessences. This is an unspeakable torture during which he needs all his faith and superhuman strength, and during which he becomes the great patient, the great criminal, the great accursed—and the great learned one!—among men. —For he arrives at the *unknown*! Because he has cultivated his own soul—which was rich to begin with—more than any other man! He reaches the unknown; and even if, crazed, he ends up by losing the understanding of his visions, at least he has seen them! Let him die charging through those unutterable, unnameable things; other horrible workers will come; they will begin from the horizons where he has succumbed!

The social and the rational side of the poet must be destroyed so that he may reach the unknown. Where the romantics found the unknown in nature, where Baudelaire placed it "behind" nature, Rimbaud located it within the self. Mallarmé, speaking of a "descent into the Self," did the same. Huysman's character, Des Esseintes, presented a fictionalized version of the extent to which the artist of this period had to withdraw, to seal himself off from the world in order to reach "the depths." If the social selves of these poets tended to manifest impotence and withdrawal, their "inner" selves did not. Rimbaud, Lautréamont, and Valéry all

[3] Bernard, 1966, pp. 9-11.

wrote seriously about the desire to be God. This "angelism" is also clearly present in Mallarmé. If God is, as Tillich (1967) suggested, the ineffable "ground of being," what Goldstein (1939) called pure experience, or *Erleben* (a quality which comes to dominate consciousness as regression deepens), then it is possible to see the psychic referent of this desire: the desire to be God is a desire to reach a deeply regressed state of consciousness. In terms of psychoanalytic theory, too, such narcissism and oceanic experiences would be expected to come to the fore with deep regression.

Poetry

The poetry of this period exhibits a good deal of oral imagery and imagery concerning original unity:

> If I have any *taste* it is hardly for anything
> But the earth and rocks.
> Dinn! dinn! dinn! dinn! Let us eat the air,
> Rocks, coal, iron.
> > *Rimbaud*, Fêtes de la faim"

> If you see me, eyes lost in paradise,
> It is when I am remembering your milk drunk long ago.
> > *Mallarmé*, "Hérodiade"

> A great black sleep
> Falls over my life:
> Sleep, all hope,
> Sleep, all desire!
> I do not see anymore.
> I lose the memory
> Of evil and of good . . .
> O the sad story!

> I am a cradle
> That a hand rocks
> In the hollow of a vault . . .
> Silence, silence!
> > *Verlaine*, "Sagesse," II, 5

Mallarmé's poetry exhibits a concern for sterile purity and coldness which, along with less frequent images of disgust reminiscent of Baudelaire (in reference to his body he speaks of the "rancid night of the skin"), suggest anal concerns. The following passage illustrates his concerns with narcissism, purity, and the "fatal woman":

> Yes, it is for me, for me, that I flower, alone!
> You know it, amethyst gardens, buried

Endlessly in learned dazzling abysses,
Hidden golds, keeping your ancient light
Under the sombre sleep of a primordial earth,
You stones wherein my eyes like pure jewels
Borrow their melodious light, and you
Metals which give to my young hair
A fatal splendour and its massive form!
. . . .
I love the horror of being a virgin and I wish
To live in the terror which my hair gives me
So that at evening, lying on my bed, inviolate
Reptile, I may feel in my vain flesh
The cold scintillation of your pale light,
You who die, you who burn with chastity,
White night of icicles and cruel snow!
                    Mallarmé, "Hérodiade"[4]

The following passage by Verhaeren illustrates extreme de-libidinalization of the external world, a trait that might be expected to accompany deep regression, since, in psychoanalytic theory, such regression is connected with withdrawal of "ca-thexes" into the self. Also note the black sun, according to Jung an index of deep regression, and the anal imagery, according to Freud another index of such regression.

The frost hardens the waters; the wind blanches the clouds.

To the east of the meadow, in the rough soil
There is, rising and shivering, the spade
Mournful and bare.

—Make a cross on the yellow soil
With your long hand,
You who depart by the road—
. . . .
Some dead toads in the infinite ruts
And some fish in the reeds
And then a cry, ever weaker and slower of a bird,
Infinitely, yonder, a cry of death
. . . .
—Make a cross over tomorrow,
Definitive, with your hand—
. . . .
For it is the end of the fields and it is the end of the evenings;
Mourning turns in the depths of the sky, like millstones,
Its black suns;

[4] Fowlie, 1953, p. 145

And only maggots bloom
In the rotten sides of women who are dead.

To the east of the meadow, in the rough soil,
On the scattered corpse of old ploughlands,
Rules there, and forever,
Plate of bright steel, lath of cold wood,
The spade.

Verhaeren, "La Bêche"

The following passage illustrates the stylistic slippage of the period, its tendency to produce images having high metaphor distance, and a good deal of associatively based thinking:

Sentimental blockade! Shipping lines of the Levant! . . .
Oh! falling of the rain! Oh! falling of the night,
Oh! the wind! . . .
All Saints' Day, Christmas, and the New Year;
Oh, in the drizzle, all my chimneys! . . . of factories. . . .
We can't sit down any more, all the benches are wet;
Believe me, it is ended till next year;
All the benches are wet, the woods have rusted so,
And so often the horns have blown, ton ton, ton taine!
. . . .
This evening a done-for sun lies on the top of the hill,
Lies on its side, in the broom, on its overcoat.
A sun white as a gob of spit in a tavern
On a litter of yellow broom,
Of yellow autumn broom.
And the horns sound for him!
That he come back. . . .
That he come back to himself!
Tally-ho! tally-ho!
O mournful anthem, have you finished! . . .
And they play the fool! . . .
And he lies there, like a gland torn out of a neck,
And he shivers, with nobody there! . . .

Laforgue, "L'Hiver qui vient"

Metaphor Distance

Saint-Pol-Roux' "Soir de Brebis" shows the extremes of metaphor distance attained by the poets of this period:

The spot of blood sets on the horizon here.
The drop of milk dawns on the horizon there.

A simple man, scattering himself in his flute and whose prudence has the shape of a black dog, the shepherd descends the hill's adolescence.

His sheep follow him, with two vine boughs for ears and two bunches of grapes for udders, his sheep follow him: walking vines.

So pure the flock! that, on this summer evening, it seems to snow childishly toward the plain.

These tiny caskets of life have, up there, grazed the perfuming pans and come down full.

Roux' comparison of the sun to a spot of blood recalls Laforgue's comparisons of it, in the passage quoted previously, to a gob of spit and a gland torn out of a neck. All these objects are similar to the sun in shape and, perhaps, in color but they are quite remote associates. The passage is full of such distant associates, but it does make sense for the most part. At first glance, Roux seems to be apprehending the concept *prudence* concretely, but he seems to mean merely that the man has prudently taken along a dog. Similarly, calling sheep *caskets* strikes one as incongruous as long as his mind is fixed upon the dominant meaning of the word. Thus, the images tend to be distant but comprehensible, something that is not the case with many surreal images.

CRISIS AND RESOLUTION

The angelism of the symbolists involved a desire to be something one cannot be. Similarly, they demanded the impossible of poetry. They tried to write down the contents and the experiences of the ineffable states of consciousness connected with deep regression. Only the German language has any sort of vocabulary for discourse on such states and, like these German words, the "words" of such regressive states are essentially untranslatable. The impossibility of the task may explain why a number of poets gave up symbolism, and even poetry itself, in disgust. Rimbaud turned to adventure in the "real" world. Valéry, having apparently confronted some regressive phenomenon he could or would not face again, gave up poetry for twenty years. Moréas, who had only six years before been the founder of the "official" school of symbolism, founded *l'Ecole romane française* in 1891. The aim of l'Ecole was a return to classicism, a return that involved the explicit rejection of the novelty criterion and of the new forms and contents of the nineteenth century. Tailhéde's feeble comparison, "The mornings were as white as doves," shows the effect of this return to the old rules.

Others wished to return only to a sentimental, humanistic pre-Baudelairean romanticism. Francis Jammes is an example:

I love in the past Clara d'Ellebeuse,
the pupil of old boarding schools,
who went, on warm evenings, beneath the linden trees
to read the *magazines* of other days.

I love only her, and I feel on my heart
the blue light of her white throat.
Where is she? Where was that happiness then?
Into her bright room some branches came.

Jammes, "J'aime dans les temps"

The freshness and sentimentality of these lines clash strongly with the delibidinalization and desolation of the selections from Laforgue and Verhaeren. Clara d'Ellebeuse does not sound at all like Mallarmé's icy, metallic Hérodiade.

Raymond (1940) has chronicled the confusion of schools rising up in response to the crisis of symbolism. The group of poets whom Raymond terms the "Fantaisistes"—Apollinaire, Salmon, and Jacob—hit upon the path destined to be followed. They allowed new content into poetry but, more important, they allowed the stylistic level of their poetry to disintegrate. It was no longer necessary for *like* to join like subjects; one did not have to search out the distant associate but could substitute for it the close but contradictory or arbitrary associate. Surprise was the key:

Surprise is the greatest source of what is new. It is by surprise, by the important position that has been given to surprise, that the new spirit distinguishes itself from all the literary and artistic movements which have preceded it. (Apollinaire, "L'Esprit nouveau et les poètes")[5]

Surprising things were to be found not inside the self, not in the depths of regression, but outside in new inventions and everyday objects:

It is Christ who ascends into the sky better than the aviators
He holds the world's altitude record
. . . .
And everything eagle phoenix and Chinese pihis
Fraternize with the flying machine

Now you walk through Paris all alone amid the crowd
Herds of bellowing busses roll by near you

Apollinaire, "Zone"

The new style allowed the poet to return to close associates and shallow regression. Along with this went an outward orientation

[5] Shattuck, 1948, p. 233.

and a freshness and zest lacking in the symbolist and decadent poets. Obviously, the poet could not write about airplanes or busses until they were invented, but the poets of the nineteenth century tended consistently to exclude the "mundane" new inventions of their day. There were no paeons to steam engines but, rather, only a few derisive comments about "dark Satanic mills." Moreover, the new content was accompanied by a loosening of rules concerning the logic of what the poet said:

> I stop to watch
> Upon the incandescent grass
> A serpent wander it is myself
> Who am the flute which I play
> And the whip which chastises the others.
> *Apollinaire,* "Les Collines"

The symbolists used "inappropriate" adjectives, but they did not say things like this. Apollinaire, without benefit of punctuation, tells us that he is a serpent that is a flute that is a whip. Clearly, the last three are close associates if one is associating on the basis of shape; it is the semantic structure into which they are fitted that leads to high metaphor distance.

SURREALISM

Theory of Poetry

Breton (1924, p. 37) defined surrealism as follows:

> Pure psychic automatism by which one proposes to express whether verbally, or in writing, or by any other means, the real functioning of thought. Dictated by thought, in the absence of all control exercised by reason, beyond all aesthetic or moral preoccupation.
>
> Surrealism rests on the belief in the superior reality of certain forms of associations neglected until now, in the all-powerfulness of the dream, of the disinterested play of thought. It tends to destroy definitively all other psychic mechanisms and to substitute these for them in the resolution of the principal problems of life.

The surrealists extended the stylistic disintegration of the previous period and seemed to begin a new regressive voyage. First, let us examine the rules set forth by Reverdy (1918), a "presurrealist," concerning the poetic image:

> The image is a pure creation of the spirit. It is not born of a comparison, but from the joining of two realities, more or less

distant. . . . An image is not good because it is brutal or fantastic, but because the association of the ideas is distant and just. . . . One creates . . . a good image, new for the mind in bringing together without comparison two distant realities of which *the mind alone* has seized the connections.

Eluard moves further; commenting on this passage he says, "If judgment approves the image, however little, it kills it."[6] Breton (1924, p. 52) moves still further: "For me, the best [image] is the one which presents the greatest degree of arbitrariness." Clearly, the rules governing degree of elaboration have been considerably loosened. The use of automatic writing—recording free-associative trains of thought without revision—in the composition of surreal poetry supports this contention.

The surrealists explicitly retained the goal of nineteenth-century poetry, the quest for *le Merveilleux*, or the Infinite and Absolute, but they sought it in the chance juxtapositions of objects in reality. They tried to look at life with fresh eyes, to see the incongruous juxtapositions of everyday life which are usually ignored. According to Aragon (1926, pp. 142-143),

Reality is the apparent absence of contradiction. The marvelous is the contradiction which appears in reality. . . . I set out to discover the face of the infinite under the concrete forms which escort me, walking the length of the streets of the earth.

If the course of nineteenth-century poetry paralleled the regressive symptoms of schizophrenia (Fenichel, 1945: world destruction fantasies, narcissism and feelings of grandeur, movement toward schizophrenic thinking), the surrealists exhibited some of the symptoms of restitution (object addiction, world reconstruction fantasies [cf. their alliance with Marxism and the desire to "change life"], and peculiarities of language). But Breton (1929, p. 76) made clear the more basic intrapsychic, regressive destination:

Everything leads me to believe that there exists a certain point in the mind where life and death, real and imaginary, past and future, communicable and uncommunicable, high and low, cease to be perceived contradictorily. Now, it is in vain that one would seek in surrealist activity any other motive than the hope of determining this point.

It would be equally vain, we might add, to seek this point in logical, secondary process thought.

---

[6] Quoted by Raymond, 1940, p. 286.

Role of Poet

Where the symbolist poets tended to be withdrawn, impotent individuals, the surrealists revived the romantic ideal of action in the world. Less regressive personalities were recruited to the role of poet, since it was not regression but lack of elaboration that was called for. In a certain sense, once one was able to learn the "trick" of not elaborating, of combining contraries, it was easy to be a surreal poet. Action in the world was stressed in two senses. First, there was the political alliance with Marxism. Second, there was the dogma of the "gratuitous act," or the surreal act which could make life itself into a poem. Breton (1929, p. 78) wrote that "the simplest surrealist act consists of, revolvers in one's hands, descending into the street and firing at random, as much as one can, into the crowd."

Poetry

The following poem by Breton illustrates the degree to which contradiction is allowed in surreal poetry:

I love you opposite the seas
Red as the egg when it's green
You move me into a clearing
Gentle with hands like a quail

. . . .
You put me to bed
By the fact of having lived
Before and after
Under my rubber eyelids
                    Breton, "Tiki"[7]

Eluard's incongruities are more subtle:

You see the bare plain on the side of the dragging sky
The snow high as the sea
And the sea high in the blue

. . . .
Foolish my true gold standards
Plains my good adventures
Useful verdure delicate cities

. . . .
I see men true sensitive good useful
Throw away a burden slighter than death
And sleep joyfully in the noise of the sun
                    Eluard, "Nous sommes"[8]

[7] Fowlie, 1955, p. 169.
[8] Fowlie, 1955, pp. 191-193.

Other surrealists have produced accounts of unreal and absurd adventures, texts that follow a certain internal logic alien to that of reality:

> When man's dam began to move, breathed in by the giant flaw of the abandonment of the divine, words in the distance, words that did not want to be lost, tried to resist the exorbitant pressure. There the dynasty of their meaning was decided.
>
> I have run to the exit of this diluvian night. Standing in the quaking dawn, with my belt full of seasons, I await you, O my friends who are about to arrive. Already I feel you behind the darkness of the horizon. My hearth's good wishes for your houses are not dried up. And my staff of cypress laughs for you with all its heart.
>
> (Char, "Seuil")[9]

Some of Michaux' productions resemble Char's, while others are more amusing:

> Stretching his hands out of the bed, Plume was amazed at not touching the wall. "Well," he thought, "the ants must have eaten it . . . " and he went back to sleep.
>
> Soon after, his wife took hold of him and shook him: "Good-for-nothing," she said, "Look! while you were busy sleeping, they stole our house from us." It was true. Wherever he looked, he saw the sky. "Bah! it's done now," he thought.
>
> Soon after, he heard a nosie. It was a train rushing at them. "With all that haste," he thought, "it will certainly get there before us," and he went back to sleep.
>
> (Michaux, "Un Homme paisible")[10]

Metaphor Distance

The surrealists tended to attain high metaphor distance by means of denotative incongruity, with contradictions, such as "seas red like the egg when it is green." Breton (1924, p. 53) quotes as a good surreal image, Soupault's

> Une église se dressait éclatante comme une cloche.
> (A church rose striking like a bell.)

Soupault connects a church and a bell because both are associated with "striking": the height of a church may be immediately striking in an emotional sense, while a bell strikes in a physical sense. "Striking" is a *close* associate of both. Similarly, green is a close associate of both sea and of red; it is the semantic articulation of the elements into a denotatively incongruous communication that leads to high metaphor distance. In contrast, the symbolists were restricted by their rules of elaboration to

[9]Hartley, 1959, p. 291.
[10]Fowlie, 1955, p. 243.

connotative incongruity. Both symbolist and surrealist were given to free-associative thought. The difference is that the symbolists thought at *deeper* levels of regression (i.e., thought more free-associatively) but, following this, elaborated their productions at *shallower* levels of regression and screened out denotative incongruity. Their poems had to make some sort of sense, no matter how arcane. Surreal poetry, on the other hand, is less elaborated, so denotative incongruity is allowed to remain and brings about greater metaphor distance than is possible with the methods of the symbolists.

Chapter 6
EXAMINATIONS OF OTHER CONTEXTS

History is, in effect, a science of complex analogies, a science of double vision.

EICHENBAUM

METAPHYSICAL POETRY

Johnson (1779) in his "Life of Cowley," defines metaphysical wit as "a kind of *discordia concors*; a combination of dissimilar images or discovery of occult resemblances in things apparently unlike." He continues, "Of wit, thus defined, they have more than enough. The most heterogeneous ideas are yoked by violence together." Metaphysical poetry as a whole, then, tended to be characterized by high metaphor distance. Williamson (1930) and Gardner (1957) note that the metaphysical poets were not professional poets but amateurs who passed their poems around within their select circle in manuscript form and seldom published them. Williamson suggests that contemporary critics were not hostile to but unaware of them. Further, they were upper middle class professionals who supported themselves by means of their extraliterary occupations; thus there was no dependence upon patronage. As Drayton scornfully put it, they were "chamber poets." It is clear that, beyond constituting an interacting autonomous system, they placed a very high value upon novelty.

Many critics have argued that it is ingenuity rather than imagination that was prized, that metaphysical poetry sprang from the conscious, rational mind rather than from the "unconscious" or regressive mind. Alvarez (1961, p. 69) makes the following statement concerning George Herbert:

> ... Herbert uses Nature always with an element of what I called "manners". Even the
>
> > Sweet rose, whose hue angrie and brave
> > Bids the rash gazer wipe his eye;
>
> for all the tenderness of the description, has a second root somewhere in the polite, social world. It behaves.

But the one thing it does not do is behave itself; just beneath the surface, the second line invites a *variorum* reading by the primary process:

> Bids the razor gash wipe his eye;

which does make sense in terms of the first line. One stumbles over *rash gazer* but not over *razor gash*. It is impossible to know whether the latter image ever inhabited Herbert's mind at any level, but it seems more likely that the roots of this poetry are in the impolite and asocial world of the primary process rather than in the socialized secondary process world. T. S. Eliot's comment that the metaphysical poets exhibited a "direct sensuous apprehension of thought, or a recreation of thought into feeling," supports this contention. Williamson (1930, p. 89) holds that this was "thinking in which the image is the body of the thought rather than a thing of beauty in itself," and goes on to say (p. 242) that for Donne abstractions become concrete and sensuous. This suggests regressive cognition, or libidinalization of thought, although accompanied, of course, by a thick rind of secondary process elaboration.

Williamson divides the metaphysical poets into a sacred and a profane line, both stemming from Donne. Based upon this division and the line of succession indicated by Williamson we may construct a sort of metaphysical chi-square (see Table 6.1).

We have argued that the metaphysical poets valued novelty and that it seems they achieved it via regression. We can predict from the theory that (1) later metaphysical poetry should exhibit more extreme metaphor distance than earlier metaphysical poetry; (2) the later poetry should exhibit more regressive imagery; (3) there may be stylistic slippage over the course of time because of the high degree of autonomy; and (4) the sacred poetry should

TABLE 6.1

Metaphysical Poets in the Sacred and Profane Series

	Profane	Sacred
Early	Lord Herbert (1583-1648) Edward King (1592-1669)	George Herbert (1593-1633)
Late	Edward Benlowes (1603-1676) John Cleveland (1613-1658) Abraham Cowley (1618-1667) Andrew Marvell (1621-1678)	Richard Crashaw (1612-1649) Henry Vaughan (1621/2-1695)

change less rapidly because of its greater meaningfulness. In gathering evidence for these predictions I have done a sort of qualitative content analysis of the comments by Williamson (1930) and Alvarez (1961) on the course of the metaphysical movement.

The Profane Series

Williamson (1930, p. 31) lists as three characteristics of Donne's conceits that they always have a rational meaning, they make sense; they draw from a wide range of material, including technical and philosophical words; and they exhibit a large "imaginative distance." He quotes Carew as saying that Donne had "drawne a line of masculine expression." Many commentators have mentioned the masculine, assertive character of Donne's verse. Alvarez (1961, p. 23) notes his high frequency of usage of words such as *for, therefore,* and *since.* Thus his verse is highly elaborated on a secondary process level, but we noted a certain "libidinalization" of thought in it.

Both high elaboration and high metaphor distance are noticeable in the following examples of early metaphysical verse:

> and your bodies print
> Like to a grave, the yielding downe doth dint.
>> *Donne*
>> "Epithelamion Made at Lincolnes Inne"[1]

> And twixt me and my soules dear wish
> The earth now interposed is,

[1] Unless otherwise indicated, the quotations follow Gardner (1957), except in the case of Crashaw, where they follow the Oxford edition of that poet's works (Martin, 1957).

Which such a strange eclipse doth make
As ne're was read in Almanake.
　　　　　　　King, "The Exequy"

This said, in her up-lifted face,
　Her eyes which did that beauty crown,
　　Were like two starrs, that having faln down,
Look up again to find their place.
　　　　　　　Lord Herbert, "Ode"

If they [our souls] be two, they are two so
　As stiffe twin compasses are two,
Thy soule the fixt foot, makes no show
　To move, but doth, if the'other doe.

And though it in the center sit,
　Yet when the other far doth rome,
It leanes, and hearkens after it,
　And growes erect, as it comes home.
　　Donne
　　"A Valediction: Forbidding Mourning"

Williamson (1930, p. 225) gives us a clue as to what happened to metaphor distance and elaboration between the early and the late period: ". . . with the deep thoughts gone, the images were simply reprehensible. Since these images had been peculiarly scientific and primarily denotative in purpose, their suggestion became shocking and ludicrous when their thoughtfulness disappeared." We may use the "correction equation" suggested in Chapter 13 for translating these qualitative comments into our quantitative terms: elaboration decayed, thus facilitating increases in metaphor distance. Of Cleveland, Williamson says, "His sole concern is to outdo his rivals in the game of conceits," and calls his verse "abstruse" and "grotesque." He uses the following terms to describe Benlowes: "most fantastic," "furor poeticus," "mystical devotion," "extravagant," and "obscure." Alvarez (1961, p. 99) notes that Cleveland and Benlowes use puns and word associations as the basis of their conceits rather than meaning, and suggests that they are just playing a "game of word-association." This further supports the notion of stylistic disintegration, of a movement toward elaboration on more regressed levels.

The following verses from Benlowes, quoted by Williamson, illustrate the stylistic disintegration of the period:

Betimes, when keen-breath'd winds, with frosty cream,
　Periwig bald trees, glaze tattling stream:
For May-games past, white-sheet *peccavi* is Winter's theme.
. . . .

Each gallon breeds a ruby; —drawer! score'um—
Cheeks dyed in claret seem o' th'quorum,
When our nose-carbuncles, like link-boys, blaze before 'um.
> *Benlowes*, "Theophila"

Other examples, the first two from Marvell and the last from Benlowes, illustrate extreme metaphor distance:

Let us roll all our Strength, and all
Our sweetness, up into one Ball:
And tear our Pleasures with rough strife,
Through the Iron gates of Life.
> *Marvell*, "To His Coy Mistress"

But now the Salmon-Fishers moist
Their Leathern Boats begin to hoist;
And, like Antipodes in Shoes,
Have shod their Heads in their Canoos.
> *Marvell*, "Upon Appleton House"

Death's serjeant soon thy courted Helens must
    Attach, whose eyes, now orbs of lust,
The worms shall feed on, till they crumble into dust.
> *Benlowes*, "Theophila"

As the quotation at the beginning of the chapter may suggest, Dr. Johnson took a dyspeptic view of what he considered Cowley's extreme incongruities. Johnson (1790, Vol. I, p. 46) was also particularly distressed by the following lines of Cleveland's:

Nay, what's the sun but, in a different name,
A coal-pit rampant, or a mine on flame!
Then let this truth reciprocally run,
The sun's heaven's coalery, and coals our sun.
> *Cleveland*, "News from Newcastle"

There seems to be an increase in regressive imagery paralleling these increases in metaphor distance and disintegrations of stylistic level, but let us turn to the sacred series of metaphysical poets, where increases in regressive imagery are much more clearcut.

The Sacred Series

We have spoken of Donne's poetry; Williamson (1930, p. 110) holds that George Herbert's poetry is more concrete and more dainty than Donne's, yet that there are touches of horror in it. In the example given in the introductory section we were at least able to read horror into it. An example of the horrific tinge to

Herbert's verse is the following:

> Only a sweet and vertuous soul,
> Like season'd timber, never gives;
> But though the whole world turn to coal,
>   Then chiefly lives.
>
> *G. Herbert*, "Vertue"

Herbert has often been compared with Henry Vaughan, his later counterpart in the sacred line; thus our work has largely been done for us. Vaughan was a solitary, unsocial poet and a genuine mystic, which suggests deep regression. T. S. Eliot (1932) comments, "In short, the emotion of Herbert is clear, definite, mature and sustained; whereas the emotion of Vaughan is vague, adolescent, fitful and retrogressive." Alvarez (1961, p. 72) claims that Vaughan "presented religious feelings as a matter of physical sensation." The following verses support the contention of deep regression:

> I saw Eternity the other night
> Like a great *Ring* of pure and endless light,
>   All calm, as it was bright.
>
> *Vaughan*, "The World"

We can conclude from these judgments that Vaughan was given to greater depths of regression than was Herbert. Deep regression is also evident in Crashaw, the other late metaphysical poet in the spiritual line. Williamson says Crashaw manifested a "voluptuous mysticism," a feminine mind, and was given to responses on the level of hearing, smell, and taste. The oral and libidinal quality of his poetry is so blatant as to leave little doubt of extreme regression:

> Loe where a wounded heart, with bleeding eyes conspire;
> Is she a flaming fountaine, or a weeping fire?
> . . . .
>   Upwards thou dost weepe,
> Heav'ns bosome drinkes the gentle streame,
>   Where the milky Rivers creepe
> Thine floates above and is the creame.
> Waters above the Heavens, what they bee,
> We'are taught best by thy Teares, and thee.
> . . . .
>   Every Morne from hence,
> A brisk Cherub something sips,
>   Whose sacred influence
> Adds sweetnes to his sweetest lips,

Then to his Musick, and his song
Tastes of his breakefast all day long.
        Crashaw, "The Weeper"

To thee these first fruits of my growing death
(For what else is my life?) lo I bequeath.
Taste this, and as thou lik'st this lesser flood
Expect a Sea, my heart shall make it good.
. . . .
Then let him drinke, and drinke, and doe his worst,
To drowne the wantonnesse of his wild thirst.
        Crashaw
        "Our Lord in His Circumcision to His Father"

In the first example, Crashaw thinks of Mary Magdalene weeping (upwards) and her tears being transmuted into cream and drunk by cherubs; in the second, Jesus offers up to God the fruits of his circumcision and invites him to eat and drink them. These examples are not atypical of Crashaw's verse: devotion is consistently depicted by licking and other forms of oral incorporation, and the most frequent adjective in his verse is probably "sweet." The examples given contain illustrations of high metaphor distance; other verses provide a more extreme instance:

They have left thee naked, Lord, O that they had!
This garment too I would they had deny'd.

Thee with thy self they have too richly clad;
Opening the purple wardrobe in thy side.

O never could there be garment too good
For thee to wear, But this, of thine own Blood.
        Crashaw
        "Upon the Body of Our Blessed Lord
        Naked and Bloody"

Based on the evidence of pervasive oral imagery in Crashaw and the comparisons between Herbert and Vaughan, it seems that regressive imagery did increase over the course of time in the sacred line of metaphysical poets. The examples from Crashaw also suggest rather extreme metaphor distance in the later periods. There does not seem to be as much stylistic slippage in this case as there was with the later profane poets, perhaps because of the greater meaningfulness and, hence, greater arousal potential of the subject matter.

MODERN PAINTING

In order to extrapolate the theory to painting, we must find new measures of elaboration, regression, and, especially, metaphor distance. Regresssion can be assessed in a fairly straightforward manner from the content of a given painting. We can measure one aspect of elaboration in terms of the closeness of the style to a photographic one. Peckham (1965) discusses discontinuity (more or less the analogue of metaphor distance) in painting in terms of deviations from the implied geometric arrangement of the contents of a painting.

There are really two parallel series constituting the history of French painting since 1800: the succession of avant-gardes, which most critics take as constituting "modern art", and the series of academic and realistic painters who have been until recently generally disregarded as having produced "atrocities." The succession of schools constituting the avant-garde series all tended to develop in an autonomous setting, although they were later accorded public and official recognition. Let us discuss the following series:

Classic: Ingres, David.
Romantic: Géricault, Delacroix.
Impressionist: Courbet, Renoir.
Expressionist: Cézanne, Van Gogh.
Cubist: Braque, Picasso.
Surreal: Matta, Masson.

As we go from the classical baseline provided by Ingres or David to the expressionists, two things seem to change: the level of elaboration, in the sense of photographic realism, disintegrates, and regressive imagery seems to increase somewhat. The romantics painted concretized emotions; their paintings are full of storms, wild landscapes, and suffering. Like the romantic poets, they seem to have projected their emotions onto the environment. The impressionists moved to the level of sensations. Finally, the painting of Van Gogh and Cézanne seems to represent a movement to a deeper physiognomic perception of the world. With cubism, there is a stylistic disintegration. Art no longer has a close relation to reality as it is perceived. With the surrealists, form disintegrates even further. Our suggestions concerning the course of avant-garde art are summarized in Figure 6.1.

If we compare the early French academic painters (such as Ingres or David) with those at the end of the nineteenth century

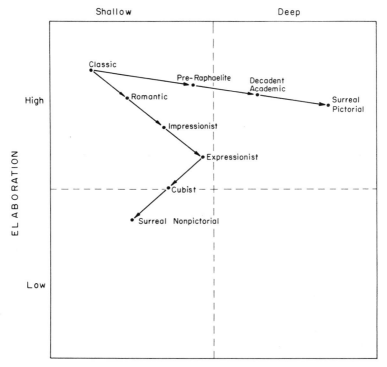

FIGURE 6.1 Schematic illustration of the course of modern painting in terms of regression and elaboration.

(such as Moreau) there is a noticeable increase across time in libidinal imagery. Moreau produced painting after painting of Salome; all of his figures have an androgynous air about them. Academic paintings of this era have a smothering, hothouse feel. Their content strikes one as more regressive and libidinous than that of contemporary impressionist and expressionist paintings. Gombrich (1956, p. 196) comments on the works of Bouguereau, ". . . he places before us a most convincing image of a nude model. Why, then, does it make us rather sick? I think the reason is obvious. This is a pin-up girl rather than a work of art. By this we mean that the erotic appeal is on the surface."

There does seem to be a definite increase in regressive imagery and some stylistic disintegration in the academic series, but what of metaphor distance? The natural poses of classical figures, as opposed to the unnatural posturing of late academic figures, suggests increases here as well. Not all realistic art has been the product of the Academy. The English pre-Raphaelites produced realistic paintings with a libidinous feel between that of early and late academic painting. In the twentieth century, one branch of surrealist painters (e.g., Dali, Ernst) has produced paintings depicting in photographic detail the twisted forms of deep regressive visions. Our conclusions concerning the course of the two series are diagrammed in Figure 6.1 (cf. Figure 3.1).

CONTEMPORARY PHENOMENA

Many contemporary phenomena in the arts seem to be products of the low regression–low elaboration syndrome. Concrete poetry and pop art exhibit little regressive imagery and are characterized by a low degree of elaboration. Do not such phenomena constitute abrogations of the novelty constraint? They do not; the trivial or the absurd represents something novel, because it has heretofore been banned from art. The theater of the absurd gives us a good example. In Ionesco's "The Bald Soprano" a husband and a wife decide that they have seen each other somewhere before; after discovering that they live on the same street, at the same number, and even in the same bedroom, they decide that it is perhaps there they have met. Further inquiry allows them to *deduce* that they are husband and wife. It seems obvious that Ionesco is commenting on the absurdity of modern life, on the difficulty of communication, on people that live together but never really know each other. In terms of the theory, however, he is doing something else. He is juxtaposing, not close and incongruous associates, as the surrealists did, but close and congruous associates. He obtains novelty by putting the obvious into his characters' mouths (e.g., by having a wife announce her name to her husband), something never done before in serious drama. Ionesco merely extends one step further what the surrealists were doing.

It may be true that an age in which people did not think that life was absurd might not patronize this sort of art, but that is not what causes the art. Those who are given to theorizing about the absurdity of the "modern condition" tend to use phenomena such as the theater of the absurd to prove their point; they infer from the theater of the absurd that life is absurd and then claim that the theater derives from life. We, on the other hand, claim that the theater of the absurd has nothing special to do with modern life, that it derives in direct fashion from the previous trend of events in art history.

On another level, we see a recapitulation of many of the trends of nineteenth-century poetry in the recent history of American popular music. Rock-and-roll music of the 1950's concerned primarily emotions and social interaction. In the music of the 1960's, there seems to be a lessening of such content and increasing references to sensations, drives, and altered states of consciousness. It is difficult to avoid a comparison with the transition from romantic to Parnassian and symbolist schools in French poetry. The incongruity of the popular music of the 1960's seems to be greater than that of the 1950's; certainly, dissonance and complexity of chords seem to have shown marked increases. It would seem, also, that average loudness has increased. All of these changes suggest attempts to counteract habituation of arousal potential. The *persona* of the performer has changed from the "Byronic" stance of, say, Elvis Presley to the frankly androgynous stance of singers such as David Bowie. Presumably, American popular music has compressed into twenty years the trends which occupied eighty or ninety in French poetry, primarily because the latter was a much more complex and difficult art form. Complexity, we have argued, should be inversely related to rate of artistic change. On the level of difficulty, the French poet labored under the weight of long tradition. His images had to be original or novel referred to this baseline. The composer of popular lyrics on the other hand must be novel only in terms of a much less stringent criterion. Certainly he does not feel compelled to outdo previous lyric poetry, since he belongs to a different tradition. He competes more or less entirely against a tradition which seldom stretches more than twenty or thirty years into the past. Because of the lack of strong institutions for preserving popular music, pressure for novelty cannot cumulate across generations in the sense that it does in poetry.

Part III
QUANTITATIVE EVIDENCE

Chapter 7
GENERAL PROCEDURE

Each art . . . passes invariably through several phases,
the order of sequence and constitutive character
of which being constant are susceptible
to a scientific study.

LALO

DESIGN

The remaining chapters describe an empirical investigation of theoretically generated hypotheses concerning changes over time in the content of poetry. Such an undertaking involves three basic problems: (1) derivation of operationalized measures from the theoretical variables; (2) definition of the population to be studied and systematic sampling from it; and (3) application of the measures to the samples. The guiding principles for each of these operations has been maximization of objectivity. Since we were interested in textual variables, the method employed was content analysis; in order to maximize objectivity, a computer-based approach was used.

In this investigation we focused on three major dependent textual variables: metaphor distance, stylistic level, and regressive imagery. These variables were operationalized in terms of content-analytic coding schemes based upon word frequencies and upon frequencies of co-occurrence of classes of words. The major theoretical independent variables were autonomy and the implicit need for originality engendered by time-in-series. Both of these were built into the design whereby subjects were selected.

105

We wanted to sample from two independent populations of poets which differed in autonomy. One high- and one low-autonomy population were selected. French poets born between 1770 and 1909 and English poets born between 1670 and 1809 were chosen as the high- and low-autonomy populations, respectively. Each of these timespans was divided into seven twenty-year periods, and three poets born within each period were objectively selected to represent the period. Finally, random samples were drawn from the poetry of each of these poets. Thus, the data analyzed consisted of samples of texts drawn from twenty-one English and twenty-one French poets.

The procedure employed in the investigation rests upon two basic tenets: objective selection of texts to be analyzed and objective methods of analysis. These principles constitute a general definition of the *content analytic method.* In any empirical investigation, we are concerned with finding evidence that can be construed as either supporting or falsifying the underlying theory. When our interest lies in the explanation of textual material we have two alternatives: we may read the texts and get an idea of their meaning, or we may utilize some quantitative method, such as counting words or themes, from which we hope to infer meaning. The second strategy would, of course, be superfluous were it possible to find out what we want to know by means of the first. However, if we are concerned with subtle differences or if we have to analyze a large number of documents, we must turn to the second method. For example, in the studies described in these chapters, over one hundred variables were investigated for forty-two poets. More than 4,200 different values thus result. However, it is not even the values themselves, but their interrelationships, which are of interest. Without some sort of quantitative mnemonic system, such an undertaking would be impossible.

Objective analysis is only one part of content analysis. Equally important is an objective means of text selection. In content analysis we are generally concerned with what is called inference to the source—that is, with inferring from a text some internal state (such as the intent behind the document or, more subtly, motivations and emotions which the source did not directly intend to convey) of the person who wrote it. Consider the question of whether Mallarmé was concerned with purity. The literary critic would support his answer by producing striking passages wherein Mallarmé has spoken of purity. The content analyst would support his by some indication of the frequency with which Mallarmé used words connoting purity. He would be concerned not only with the frequency of these references but also with their distribution throughout Mallarmé's writings. The subjective analyst tends to base his conclusions upon intensity of utterance while often ignoring the possibility that his few examples may be idiosyncratic. The objective analyst usually relies upon cumulative frequencies throughout texts; he is thus more able to pick up subtle preoccupations which may, in the end, outweigh more strikingly obvious ones. Above all, the content analyst would not base his interpretations upon the most well known poems of Mallarmé, but rather upon random or representative samples from all of his poems: "key" or "important" poems may be labeled such as much because they support a given theory as because they tell anything about the central concerns of the poet.

SELECTION OF SAMPLES

Populations

English poetry from ca. 1700 to ca. 1840 and French poetry from ca. 1800 to ca. 1940 were the foci of interest. Each was divided into seven twenty-year periods, each period being represented by randomly selected texts from three poets. Thus, the works of twenty-one English and twenty-one French poets were analyzed. There were several reasons for selecting these two timespans. First, we wanted two series that represented both different cultures and different eras so there would be no direct influence. (It is, for example, the first English period and the first French period that are compared, not contemporary English and French periods. There were, of course, interchanges between the later English periods and the earlier French periods.) Second, each of the series starts with the last generation of a "classical" period and hypothetically runs through a period of major stylistic change. We wanted two samples of differing autonomy (freedom from audience control). The English series tends, at least in the eighteenth century, to have slight autonomy, while in the French series autonomy is great. Since translations were used, the French series constituted the one most completely available in English. Also, French poetry, especially after the romantic period, is generally recognized as being in the vanguard of change. To have taken, say, English poetry written between 1800 and 1940 would have opened the possibility of the objection that the changes should be explained, not by internal evolution, but merely by imitation of French models.

Although a good deal has been written about literary generations and their timespans, there was no overwhelming theoretical rationale for the choice of twenty-year eras. We merely felt that twenty-five- or fifty-year periods would lead to a too gross organization of data, while periods of less than twenty years would eventuate in too subtle divisions. Certainly, there is no lack of claims that twenty-year periods approximate the "natural" divisions for the study of literary generations (cf. Michaud, 1950). At any rate, the resultant groupings of poets do fit well with the conventionally defined schools and movements.

While we were interested in periods representing the flourishing of the poets under consideration, it soon became apparent that assignment to such periods is highly subjective. An author often does the disservice of writing for more than twenty years. One is then left with the problem of deciding which period contains his important or, worse, representative works. Such decisions are always possible, but making them for all of the forty-two poets in our samples would only have led to a cumulation of errors and misjudgments. Thus we were forced back onto birthdates as a method of assignment. As Thibaudet has apologetically but truthfully observed, this is our *"seul fait donné."* Twenty-year periods beginning with 1670 for the English and 1770 for the French series were, then, set up. These periods according to birth give us periods of flourishing beginning very roughly thirty years later in each case—i.e., a series of periods beginning with 1700 and 1800 for the two samples.

Selection of Poets

Three poets were selected to represent each of the periods. From the appropriate Oxford Anthology of Verse (Hayward, 1964; Lucas and Jones, 1957; and Smith, 1926) the three poets born within each period who were assigned the largest number of pages were selected. This procedure, of course, leads to the selection of the three poets considered by the editors of the Oxford anthologies to be the most eminent or important in the period. The Oxford anthologies were used for two reasons: their widespread use and the certain authority accorded them, and the fact that anthologies covering all periods of interest are included in the series. Cross-checking with other anthologies shows that there is general agreement on the poets included and the attention devoted to them.

Selection by eminence serves several very pragmatic ends. It leads to samples that are similar to those discussed by other literary historians. It would be a conceivable project to obtain a reasonably complete list of "all" poets for each period and to select one's poets from it in some random fashion. However, one would end with a series of poets unrelated to that which others see as constituting literary history. Even given that one could compile a reasonably complete list of the population of poets, it would be most difficult to obtain a parallel set of texts from which to sample. Since, in the present study, eminence is used within short periods rather than, say, over the span of a century, arbitrary decisions concerning the importance of different styles on the part of the editors of the anthologies are eliminated to a large extent. We have selected the three poets with the largest numbers of assigned pages in each of seven different periods. In this manner that component of eminence arising from a poet's belonging to a movement currently in fashion is largely removed, leaving as a remainder the component arising from more objective considerations.

Several deviations from the general method of selecting poets occurred. In period F1, Marceline Desbordes-Valmore was not included since her inclusion would have made her the only female poet to be sampled. It was decided beforehand to limit the inquiry to male poets since theoretical analyses of creativity are aimed largely at them. André Chénier was substituted for Desbordes-Valmore. Although he was born in 1762, only two other poets were included in the anthology for the period 1770–1789 and these were already included in the sample. In period F2, Nerval was substituted for Vigny, for whom a lack of adequate translated texts existed. In two other cases—Millevoye and Musset—literal prose translations by myself were used, as no adequate translations were available, either for the two poets in question or for possible substitutes. In all cases the criterion for the existence of translations was presence in Widener Library at Harvard University. In period E7, John Clare was substituted for Tennyson. At the time of the substitution it was planned to continue the English series through several additional periods. Since Tennyson was born in the last year of E7 and since he belongs with the second generation romantics rather than with the first, he was to have appeared in period E8. In period E4, James Beattie was substituted for Charles Churchill. Satirical verse was excluded from the samples, and virtually all of Churchill's poetry is satirical. In all cases, substitutions were based upon the eminence criterion. That is, the substituted poet was the one in the period with the largest number of pages after the eliminated poet. The poets composing the final sample are listed in Table 7.1.

Selection of Editions

Once poets were chosen, it was necessary to select editions of their works to be used as a basis for sampling of texts. Criteria, in order of importance, for these selections were as follows:

1. Completeness. In all cases, the primary desideratum was to obtain as nearly as possible the complete "population" of the author's poems. It was possible to sample from the English poets' complete works in almost all cases.

2. Literalness of translation. This, of course, applies only to the French poets. Generally, the translator's preface gave an indication of the attitude toward literalness. In no case were imitations, avowedly loose, or spirit- rather than letter-following translations employed.

3. Chronological ordering of poems. This criterion allowed the composition of a subsample of poets for whom changes over time within each poet could be examined. Dating by time of composition (as opposed to time of publication) was followed.

The criteria were sufficient for narrowing the selection to one book for the French poets. In the case of the more eminent English poets this was often not true. In such cases, considerations such as legibility and ease of handling for keypunching were the deciding factors. Martindale (1969) provides a list of the editors used.

Selection of Texts

We now turn to the actual method of selection of textual samples. As the first step in each case fifty page numbers were selected from a table of random numbers. If possible, only odd-numbered pages were used, for convenience in keypunching. In double-column pages the right-hand column was always used. Approximately the first eight lines from each of these pages were keypunched. The length was allowed to vary from six to ten lines for very long or very short verse lengths. No reference was made to meaning in deciding the length of each passage. Rather, eight lines were counted and the passage was cut off at the nearest punctuation mark.

The following types of productions were *never* included in the textual samples:

TABLE 7.1

Poets Included in the Study

English series	French series
Period E1 (born 1670-1689)	Period F1 (born 1770-1789)
1. Isaac Watts	1. André Chénier
2. John Gay	2. Pierre-Jean de Béranger
3. Alexander Pope	3. Charles-Hubert Millevoye
Period E2 (born 1690-1709)	Period F2 (born 1790-1809)
4. John Byrom	4. Alphonse de Lamartine
5. James Thomson[a]	5. Victor Hugo[a]
6. John Dyer	6. Gérard de Nerval[a]
Period E3 (born 1710-1729)	Period F3 (born 1810-1829)
7. Thomas Gray	7. Alfred de Musset[a]
8. William Collins	8. Théophile Gautier[a]
9. Christopher Smart	9. Charles Baudelaire
Period E4 (born 1730-1749)	Period F4 (born 1830-1849)
10. William Cowper[a]	10. Stéphane Mallarmé
11. James Beattie	11. Paul Verlaine[a]
12. William Mickle	12. Tristan Corbière
Period E5 (born 1750-1769)	Period F5 (born 1850-1869)
13. Thomas Chatterton	13. Jean-Arthur Rimbaud
14. William Blake[a]	14. Emile Verhaeren[a]
15. Robert Burns	15. Jules Laforgue[a]
Period E6 (born 1770-1789)	Period F6 (born 1870-1889)
16. William Wordsworth[a]	16. Paul Valéry
17. Samuel Coleridge[a]	17. Guillaume Apollinaire[a]
18. Lord Byron[a]	18. Jules Supervielle[a]
Period E7 (born 1790-1809)	Period F7 (born 1890-1909)
19. Percy Shelley[a]	19. Paul Eluard[a]
20. John Clare[a]	20. Henri Michaux[a]
21. John Keats[a]	21. René Char

[a]Included in the Early-Late subsample. Remaining poets included in Odd-Even subsample.

1. Prose of any sort besides "prose poems."
2. Satirical poems.
3. Translations and imitations.
4. Explicitly labeled juvenilia.
5. First drafts, variorum readings and fragments of poems appearing elsewhere in finished form.

When page numbers containing any of the above were drawn from the table of random numbers, they were skipped and the next number used.

In general the texts were keypunched in the original form. However, some editing was necessary:

1. All contractions were spelled out.

2. Proper modern words were substituted for infrequent archaic and dialectical words. Frequent words of this type (e.g., *thine, swain*) were, if appropriate, included in the dictionary and thus did not need editing.

3. Sentence delimiters (+) were substituted for the following punctuation marks: ; : ? !. Thus, each was treated as if it were a period. This rule was followed in all cases except such archaic usages as, "Oh! hello."

4. Where no punctuation was used by a poet (Apollinaire and some poems by Eluard) a naive assistant was asked to supply sentence delimiters according to the sense of the passages.

5. Since an analysis of the presentation of sexual roles was made (on the French sample only) it was necessary that each reference to males or females be made explicit. This necessitated the addition of subscripts to indefinite pronouns: e.g., *you/M, thy/F*. Such subscripts were not added to the *I* of lyric poetry nor to animals or inanimate objects which may previously have been referred to as *he* or *she*. Any such prior references were not, however, deleted.

For each of the forty-two poets, fifty samples of about eight lines each, or approximately four hundred lines of poetry, were obtained. One further step was taken. For each poet, two documents were created. These were used for the assessment of odd–even reliability and for testing hypotheses concerning changes in style and content over time *within* individual poets. The basis for the creation of one or the other type of division was the presence of an adequate chronology. Where dating was *not* present in the book used, the poet was assigned to the Odd–Even group. Here each of the fifty samples for the poet was alternatively put into an odd and an even document. Where dating was present, the fifty samples were divided at their median year of composition and the first twenty-five put into an *early* document and the last twenty-five into a *late* document for the poet. In all other analyses the two documents for each poet were merged and their mean value on the variable under consideration was used. Table 7.1 indicates the division of poets into Odd–Even and Early–Late groups.

Characteristics of the Samples

The total sample consisted of 127,695 words and 8,646 sentences. The mean number of words per poet was 3,040.4 (*SD* =

295.1). The mean number of sentences per poet was 205.9 (SD = 37.1). Kruskal-Wallis analyses of variance on ranks show that number of words or sentences per document does not differ significantly across periods for either series, nor do the French and the English series differ significantly on number of words or sentences per document.

METHOD

The General Inquirer

The General Inquirer (Stone et al., 1966; Stone and Kirsch, 1968) is a set of programs developed by Stone and his associates for computerized content analysis. The system can be used with any text and any dictionary. The details of the method are given in the references provided. Here is a simplified outline of the procedures followed in the present investigation:

1. Text to be analyzed is keypunched onto IBM cards with only the editing described in the section above.

2. A dictionary is prepared. The "Regressive Imagery Dictionary" used in the present investigation is composed of a number of "tags" (e.g., Oral imagery), each of which is made up of the words which are to be taken as indicating the presence of the tag.

3. Tagging phase. The dictionary and the text to be analyzed are processed together with the tagging program on a computer. The program, by a process of dictionary lookup and matching, attaches tags to text sentences containing words which indicate the tag. The program contains subroutines which remove suffixes so that root words may be matched with dictionary entries.

4. Tag tally. A listing by document of both the raw frequencies and the percentages (based on number of words in this case) of each of the categories or tags is produced as the final output.

The Regressive Imagery Dictionary

Most of the variables discussed in Chapters 8–14 are based upon the Regressive Imagery Dictionary constructed specifically for this study. This dictionary contains 5,336 words which are categorized into sixty-eight nonoverlapping tags. It also contains routines for tabulating seventeen scores based upon co-occurrence patterns of two or more tags within sentences. The dictionary provides empirical measures of the major theoretical constructs (e.g., metaphor distance, stylistic level, and regression). In each case derivation of appropriate measures of these constructs involved several steps: determination of which attributes of each construct were amenable to content analytic measurement, analysis of these attributes into their basic components, and determination of words which would logically be expected to indicate these components. For example, regressive cognition is theoretically expected to contain more references to drives than are contained in secondary process cognition; there are several types of drive imagery (i.e., oral, anal, sexual); finally, each of these is indicated by a set of words.

The assumption is that individual words at least indirectly indicate the depth at which a passage was inspired. Here we are concerned only with connotations and not at all with denotations in that we are interested not in *what* is said but in inferring the "mental level" at which it was conceived. When Crashaw loads his verse with words such as *drink* and *suck* we feel justified in an attribution of some importance to orality in his thought.

A problem arises with this approach in the case of such automatisms as "he hit upon the truth." In automated content analysis the *hit* may result in the scoring of aggressive imagery for this sentence. Fortunately, poets are not given to cliches, but such idiomatic usages are a problem. In the Regressive Imagery Dictionary there are a few mechanisms for avoiding the most frequent of such misattributions. In most cases such potentially troublesome words have simply been excluded from the dictionary. It is important to realize that a good deal of imprecision is involved in a study such as the present one, but the large amount of text tends to cancel out such mistagging.

Once the set of tags, or categories, had been decided upon, it was necessary to obtain a list as exhaustive as possible of words with which to fill each one. In automated content analysis it is necessary to specify each word one wishes to include in a tag since, of course, the computer has no powers of generalization. Three sources were used in the construction of the dictionary. First, Roget's *Thesaurus* (1960) provided the basic words in each category. Second, a number of previously compiled General Inquirer dictionaries were consulted. Those from which words were borrowed were as follows: *Alcohol Dictionary* (Kalin, Davis, and McClelland, 1966), *Harvard III Psychosociological Dictionary* (Stone et al., 1966), *Icarian Dictionary* (Ogilvie, 1968),

Psychoactive Drug Study Dictionary (Dinkel, n.d.), *Santa Fe Third Anthropological Dictionary* (Colby, 1966), *Stanford Political Dictionary* (Holsti, 1966). The third stage in dictionary construction was the taking of a Key Word in Context (KWIC) sample. A KWIC program transforms textual input into a listing of each word in the input, together with a few words of surrounding context which can be alphabetically sorted. The resulting printed output gives a listing of all words in the input sample together with enough context to determine whether a word can be included in simple form in one's dictionary, whether some strategy for separating different usages must be employed, or whether the word is used in so many ways that it is best left out of the dictionary.

Our smallest unit of analysis is the tag. Each contains and is defined by a set of words. Application of the dictionary to the text samples yields figures (both as raw frequencies and as percentages of number of words) concerning the frequency of the tags in each document. Each tag is independent in that any word is assigned to only one tag. However, we are generally interested in fluctuations, not of individual tags, but of groups of tags, or *categories*. For example, our interest will not be in whether a document contains a high frequency of references to visual sensations or to auditory ones but, rather, in the frequency of references to sensations of any kind. Furthermore, such references are of real interest to us only as they enter into a *summary variable* measuring regression. In general, then, we are concerned with three levels of variables:

1. Tags: composed of sets of words.
2. Categories: composed of combinations of tags.
3. Summary Variables: composed of combinations of categories.

We have followed a principle of equal weighting in moving from one level to another. Each tag is given equal weight in forming a category. Simple addition of the tag frequencies would be influenced by the number of words in a tag and by the baseline frequencies of the tags. For example, if one were to obtain a measure of frequency of sensations for a document by simply summing percentage figures for references to visual sensations and odor, he would end up with a figure which overweighted the former. There are more words connoting vision than odor and they have a higher baseline of usage. For our purposes, a doubling in the frequency of odor words is more significant than, say, a 10 percent increment in the usage of vision words, but it might not show up as such without equal weighting. For this reason, tag percentage frequencies were converted to *T*-scores. This transformation led to the creation of scores standardized with reference to the mean and standard deviation of the entire sample of forty-two poets. The *T*-score is based upon the more well-known *z*-score: by addition of and multiplication by constants a distribution is created with a mean of 50 and a standard deviation of 10:

$$z_i = \frac{x_i - \bar{x}}{SD}$$

$$T_i = 10(z_i + 5)$$

Thus all tag scores are expressed as *T*-scores and category scores are expressed as sums of *T*-scores. Operations for obtaining summary variables are discussed in later chapters; again the principle of equal weighting was followed. In order to avoid confusion, in the following chapters tag and category names are capitalized: *Sensation* refers to the content analysis category while *sensation* refers to the phenomenon itself.

Computerized content analysis has the advantage of perfect reliability in the usual senses of the term: test–retest and inter-rater reliabilities are both 1.00. Evidence concerning two other sorts of reliability of the measures derived from the Regressive Imagery Dictionary is presented in Martindale (1969). *Category consistency* (tendency of tags composing a category to intercorrelate) and *tag stability* (tendency of a tag to distribute itself evenly throughout documents from a single source) are both shown to be adequately high. Evidence concerning validity is presented in later chapters.

Other Computer Procedures

A program written by the author, SEMIS, represents an attempt to get around the difficulty, inherent in content analysis procedures, of inferring intensity of meaning from frequency of usage. The program operates on keypunched text and employs suffix removal and dictionary lookup procedures. However, instead of only categorizing words, the dictionary contains a list of words, each assigned a weight on each of up to four categories, or dimensions. The program produces the mean value on each of the dimensions of the words in a document that were found in the dictionary. The dictionary was based on norms for 925 nouns rated on seven point scales as to abstractness–concreteness, gathered by Paivio, Yuille, and Madigan (1968). These norms also contain figures concering Noble's (1952) *m*, or associative meaningfulness (the number of associations given to a word in a fixed amount of time). Each dictionary entry contains the average concreteness rating and the mean number of associations given to the word by Paivio, Yuille, and Madigan's subjects. Further details are given in Chapters 8 and 10, where the applications of these measures are discussed. A second program written by the author, LEXSTAT, was used in obtaining the measures of lexical diversity, such as the type–token ratio, discussed in Chapter 8.

USE OF TRANSLATIONS

It might be argued that the use of translations for the French series compromises the validity of the study. However, since one of our basic interests lies in comparison of the French and English texts, it is obvious that *something* had to be translated. Construction of a parallel French language Regressive Imagery Dictionary would merely have involved translating the dictionary, rather than the texts. As such, any objections which could be directed against use of translated texts would still remain. However, a methodological "defect" in the content-analytic approach allays fears of serious distortion because of use of translations. The dictionary suffers from a universal inadequacy of content analysis: frequency of words is used to measure the intensity of the inferred trait. Thus, *annoy*, *enrage*, and *kill* all have equal weights in measuring aggressive feeling. The broadness of categories in the dictionary has the advantage of allowing analysis of texts from the French series in translated form. In effect, the dictionary treats a wider range of words as cognates than is likely to be the case with any translator. So long as the translator does not leave out passages, little distortion is likely. Since the dictionary equates everything from *kill* to *reprove* in scoring aggressive imagery and includes a large number of words, translators are not likely to be able consistently to translate any words denoting an angry response in such a way that they will not be tagged.

More caution must be used in assessing the measures based on SEMIS and LEXSTAT. However, there is some evidence that even such seemingly language-specific characteristics as word length are not totally lost with translation. Herdan (1966) computed an analogue of the correlation coefficient on the relationship between number of syllables in original and translated versions of a document. For French to English translations he obtained a correlation of .51. While this is far from a perfect retention of information, a moderately strong relationship is suggested. A small consolation is offered by the fact that more information is retained in French to English translation than in the other languages studied by Herdan. Czech to English and Russian to English translations yield coefficients of .40 and .33 respectively.

STATISTICAL PROCEDURES

In the following chapters, data analysis is in almost all cases based upon nonparametric procedures. Because of large inter-period differences in variability, assumptions for parametric analysis of variance techniques were not met. Thus, fluctuations across periods were generally assessed with Kruskal–Wallis one-way analyses of variance (H). In general, Mann–Whitney U tests (U) have been used to assess interperiod differences and Sign tests (x) to assess the differences between variables. Unless otherwise noted, Spearman correlations (r_s) are reported. Siegel (1956) provides a discussion of these techniques. Because of the variability of the data and the small sample sizes, the .10 level has been taken as statistically significant. In most cases, mean values for each period are reported. The reader interested in a particular poet is referred to Martindale (1969), where individual values for most of the variables are tabulated.

Chapter 8
METAPHOR DISTANCE

*It is of the fruitful union of the grotesque and
the sublime that modern genius is born.*

HUGO

Metaphor distance is defined in general terms as the probability of the co-occurrence of the elements in any statement. More narrowly, we have used it to refer to the probability of the combination of elements in metaphors and similes. Clearly, such probabilities exist but, just as clearly, they would be difficult to determine with any degree of accuracy. Three problems would confront any attempt at a direct operationalization, such as having subjects rate retrieved similes. First, it would not be possible to retrieve enough comparisons all involving any one element to obtain reliable results, and rating across different elements would prove difficult. Second, the extremely low probabilities of poetic similes in general would make fine discriminations difficult. Third, the probabilities are influenced by their specific contexts.

INCONGRUOUS JUXTAPOSITIONS

If poets experience a need, as we have argued, to increase the intensity of incongruity (in other words, to decrease the predictability or probability of their statements), this need ought to show up on the level of *frequency* as well. Let us define an empirical measure, *Incongrous Juxtapositions*, as the frequency with which incongruous words (e.g., *good* and *evil*) occur within the same sentence in a text. Incongruous Juxtapositions taps incongruity whether or not a simile or metaphor is actually present. This expands the sample of juxtapositions in which incongruity is measured. The justification for such a procedure is that theoretically the inspirational source of poetry is associative juxtapositions; whether these appear in poetry as metaphors or similes or in some more discursive form is a function of secondary elaboration.

Incongruous Juxtapositions is, at best, an approximate operationalization of the concept of metaphor distance; it taps frequency while metaphor distance refers to the distance between the elements joined or the probability of their being joined. This, and the fact that juxtapositions must be rather obvious to be picked up in machine scoring, make Incongruous Juxtapositions a rather gross measure. Verses like

> her *fault* and *beauty*
> Blended together, show like leprosy,
> the *whiter*, the *fouler.*
>> *Webster*
>> *The Duchess of Malfi,* III, iii*

exhibit Incongruous Juxtapositions obvious even to a computer. On the other hand, Donne's comparison of lovers to a compass or Bishop King's conceit,

> But Heark! My Pulse like a soft Drum
> Beats my approach, tells Thee I come;
> And slow howere my marches be,
> I shall at last sit down by Thee.
>> *King,* "The Exequy"

(wherein his life-giving pulse is compared to a drum beating out the slow, solemn march toward death) while they exhibit infinitely greater metaphor distance, would not be picked up, since they depend upon the meaning of the sentence, rather than upon the connotations of the individual words.

Incongruous Juxtapositions works at all because of a tendency for both types of incongruity to correlate. There is a high baseline of incongruity in all poetry. Table 8.1 illustrates the correlations in our samples between tags tapping polar opposites. Note that all of the correlations are *positive* and that more than half of them are significantly so. These correlations are based upon co-occurrence within the same document, rather than within the

*Italics added.

TABLE 8.1

Correlations between Tags Measuring
Opposite Qualities

Correlation between	r
Hard–Soft	.19
Active–Passive	.27*
Strong–Weak	.02
Good–Bad	.37**
Ascend–Descend	.28*
Height–Depth	.51***
Fire–Water	.52***
Fire–Cold	.23
Positive Emotion–Anxiety	.22
Chaos–Order	.15
Diabolic–Angelic	.26*

Note. Two-tailed tests of significance.
$*p < .10.$
$**p < .05.$
$***p < .01.$

same sentence; still, the relationships are striking and support our argument for the central importance of incongruity in poetry.

It may be objected that, since contradiction is one of the qualities of regressive thought, we are merely measuring regression from a new perspective with Incongruous Juxtapositions. However, it will be remembered that regression is theoretically only *one* of the ways for achieving high metaphor distance. If Incongruous Juxtapositions is in fact merely another measure of regression, it will follow the regression curve over time rather than increasing continuously as predicted.

We are interested in the co-occurrence of four sets of polar categories: Strong-Weak, Good-Bad, Active-Passive, and Approach-Avoidance. Five tags were included in the dictionary especially to form the basis of the Incongruous Juxtapositions categories. These are: Strong, Weak, Good, Bad, and Active. As well, a number of tags used in other aspects of the investigation were used. This does not compromise the independence of Incongruous Juxtapositions, since these tags are of interest only in terms of patterns of co-occurrence. The statistical operations performed in arriving at an index of Incongruous Juxtapositions partial out any effect of the actual frequency of these tags.

The reason for the inclusion of such broad ranges of tags lies in the nature of the phenomena. Osgood conceives of *all* words as occupying some position in semantic space. What has been attempted here is an inclusion of words which would tend to occupy polar positions. Rather than being exhaustive, the specially prepared categories, such as Strong, include words not included in other tags. Thus, for example, Glory should in this context be thought of as a subclass of Strong.

The categories, component tags, and five most frequent words in each are as follows:

Strong
Strong: god, could, king, power, father.
Hard: rock, stone, hard, glass, iron.
Glory: great, gold, golden, pride, divine.

Weak
Weak: child, little, lose, poor, cannot.
Soft: soft, gentle, tender, murmur, whisper.
Anxiety: fear, tremble, dread, terror, blush.
Sadness: tears, sad, pain, weep, woe.

Good
Good: good, home, church, worth, fine.
Angelic: white, pure, pale, sacred, angel.
Moral Imperatives: should, right, virtue, honor, law.

Bad
Bad: bad, crime, shame, wrong, false.
Diabolic: black, dark, fate, curse, hell.
Anality: sweat, rot, dirty, disgust, filth.

Active
Active: wind, spirit, run, free, storm.
Aspire: wish, want, desire, dare, need.
Random Movement: wave, roll, spread, swell, shake.
Ascend: hope, rise, fly, throw, flight.

Passive
Passive: lie, death, dead, die, bed.

Approach
Love: love, friend, dear, kind, pity.
Social Behavior: say, tell, call, speak, meet.

Avoidance
Aggression: break, war, beat, strike, wound.

Within each pair of categories, the co-occurrence in the same sentence of *any* of the tags on the left with *any* of the tags on the right is scored as an incongruous juxtaposition. *Sentences* are used as the basis for percentages. Only one juxtaposition of each type may be counted per sentence. Although there may be two strong and two weak words, only one Strong–Weak juxtaposition is counted. However, the same sentence may contain juxtapositions of other types.

Several steps were involved in obtaining the final co-occurrence scores for each of the four types of juxtaposition. The number of Incongruous Juxtapositions is obviously dependent upon the basal frequencies of the elements combined. One expects a certain number of juxtapositions by chance alone. In order to control for this, for each document, the observed percentage frequency of juxtapositions (A ∩ B) was divided by the expected percentage frequency (A × B). Finally, each of the four types of juxtaposition scores, thus corrected, were converted to T-scores. The summary variable, Incongruous Juxtapositions, was obtained in two steps. First, the four juxtaposition categories in T-score form were summed. Second, since this sum was correlated with number of sentences (r_s = .32, p < .05) a deviation score for Incongruous Juxtapositions partialing out this relationship was obtained. It is this score that is henceforth referred to as Incongruous Juxtapositions.

For the periods under consideration, we may derive from the theory the prediction that Incongruous Juxtapositions will increase continuously over the entire timespan of each series. Because of the greater autonomy of the French series, we should expect the rate of change to be greater in that series. The prediction of increasing Incongruous Juxtapositions follows from the theoretical proposition that there is a constant pressure for novelty and, hence, a need to expand metaphor distance. However, this need is important in proportion to the lack of externally imposed constraints and purposes. Thus, the relative autonomy of a poetic culture is vital in determining metaphor distance and its rate of increase.

For the French series the Spearman rank correlation between time-in-series (rank, based upon birthdates, from 1 to 21) and Incongruous Juxtapositions is .53 (p < .01), while for the English it is .21 (*ns*). The slope of the regression line for the French series is appreciably steeper than that for the English, indicating a higher rate of change (t = 1.24, p → .10 for the difference between slopes). Incongruous Juxtapositions exhibits a slight tendency to level off and decline after period F4 and a clear-cut tendency in this direction after period E3. These periods of leveling off are followed in both cases by sharp increases in Incongruous

Juxtapositions in periods E7 and F7. It may be that these periods of leveling off are due to increasing difficulty of increasing metaphor distance via increasing the depth of regression. We should expect pressure for stylistic change to increase as an inverse function of the rate of increase of Incongruous Juxtapositions. This possibility is discussed in later chapters.

ASSOCIATIVE MEANINGFULNESS

In their search for incongruous juxtapositions, poets theoretically move outwards on the associative hierarchies around words. The ease with which this can be done varies. Some words seem to be surrounded by steep hierarchies; that is, they generally provoke only a few responses. Other words are surrounded by flatter hierarchies. They are bonded with greater average strength to a larger number of associates. To the extent that making remote associations to words is important for a poet, he should gravitate toward words surrounded by flatter hierarchies, since they allow for easier production of such associates. This movement would also foster greater metaphor distance in another way. By composing metaphors or similes which join words, each having a large number of associates, the poet increases the basal probability that some of these associates will be incongruous. That is, the possibilities for ambiguity and multiple interpretations are multiplied.

Verlaine suggested this very strategy, as well as a related one, in the verses quoted in Chapter 5:

. . . you must not
Choose your words without some obscurity:
Nothing more dear than the grey song
Where the Vague joins the Precise.
Verlaine, "Art poétique"

In the context of our discussion, this may be seen as a call for verse composed of words with many associates, with a few words of just the opposite type thrown in, presumably for the sake of incongruity or contrast.

Noble (1952) has defined associative meaningfulness, or m, as the average number of associates elicited by a word in a fixed amount of time. Now words with large numbers of easily accessible associates should exhibit high values of Noble's m. We may predict from the theory that the average value of associative meaningfulness of the words used in both French and English poetry should increase over time. This increase should be faster in the French series because of its greater autonomy. Since, as Verlaine suggests, juxtapositions of the vague and the precise are another method of increasing novelty, we may also predict that variability in the associative meaningfulness of words should also increase over time, again at a faster rate in the French than in the English series.

Paivio, Yuille, and Madigan (1968) have gathered normative values of Noble's m for 925 English nouns. The program SEMIS was used to apply these norms to the texts. The program gave as output the average values of the text words found in the dictionary. It also computed, for each poet, the standard deviation of the m values of these words. The first value allows us to examine changes over time in associative meaningfulness while the second allows us to examine changes in the variability of this index.

For the English series, the Spearman correlation between time-in-series and average associative meaningfulness is .43 ($p <$ .05) while for the French series it is .46 ($p < .05$). Thus, the poets in both series move toward usage of words with larger numbers of associates, although the predicted difference in the rate of this movement does not emerge. The partial correlation (holding constant changes in mean associative meaningfulness) between time-in-series and the standard deviation of associative meaningfulness is $< -.05$ (*ns*) for the English series and .43 ($p < .05$) for the French. Thus, variability in meaningfulness increases over time more quickly in the French series than in the English, where it does not increase at all. No noticeable flattenings in rate of change, such as were noted with Incongruous Juxtapositions, are seen with associative meaningfulness. This and the lack of differences between French and English rates of change suggest that it is a grosser measure of metaphor distance. Certainly, it is a less direct one. That trends in the predicted direction are found at all in this application of present-day norms to past verbal material, some of it translated, is gratifying.

LINGUISTIC DIVERSITY

While we have stressed the seeking of originality on the level of metaphor distance, which involves juxtapositions of two or more words, it would seem a reasonable extrapolation that the poet might seek novelty in other ways. He could increase diversity on the level of the individual word or sentence. Thus, he could avoid repetition of the same word or of words or sentences of the same length, and so on. In light of the theory, we might expect increases in such indices of linguistic diversity over time. It should be emphasized, however, that the theory is cast in terms of "transitional" probabilities between elements rather than in terms of the probabilities of the elements themselves. There is reason to believe that the mode of obtaining poetic novelty, regression, allows remote association and incongruous juxtapositions; there is much less reason to believe that it fosters diversity of elements.

There are a number of fairly standard indices of linguistic variability (cf. Herdan, 1966). Most are based on diversity of word usage. The hapax legomena percentage is the percentage of words which are used only once in a text. The type-token ratio is obtained by dividing the number of different or unique words (*types*) by the total number of words (*tokens*) in a text. In both cases, larger values indicate greater diversity.

Information theory (Shannon and Weaver, 1948) provides another approach to the measurement of lexical diversity. H, or first-order entropy, is computed as follows:

$$H = - \sum_{i=1}^{N} p_i \log_2 p_i$$

where N is the number of word types in a document and p_i is the probability of each. H is a measure of the amount of uncertainty in a text, but is dependent upon the number of word types in that text. In order to correct for this, we may compute

$$\text{Relative information} = \frac{H}{H_{\max}}$$

where $H_{\max} = -\log_2 \left(\frac{1}{N} \right)$

$H_{\max}$ gives the maximum information which the text could transmit. As may be inferred from the formula, information is maximal when all types occur with equal frequency. Relative information, then, gives uncertainty per unit (token) of text referred to this baseline. Larger values indicate greater relative unpredictability.

Yule's (1944) K gives a measure of the repeat rate of vocabulary usage. It is computed as follows:

$$K = 10^4 \cdot \frac{\Sigma X^2 - \Sigma X}{(\Sigma X)^2}$$

where X is the frequency of occurrence of a given word type. Kučera and Francis (1967) extrapolate K to distributions of word and sentence length. Higher values of K indicate greater amounts of repetition of the variables in question. All of these indices were computed for the textual samples using LEXSTAT.

Results are presented in Table 8.2. Given the seeming reasonableness of the prediction, the results are of interest, since they generally contradict it. Though there are some exceptions, the trend over time in both series seems to be toward less diversity. Where the correlations reach significance, they uniformly point in this direction.

We suggested that regressive states of consciousness may be conducive to the production of incongrous juxtapositions, but not to the production of discourse marked by diversity of elements. This is illustrated by the child, who hypothetically exists on a "regressed" or developmentally primitive level. Childish utterances may be surprising or incongruous but they are composed from a limited vocabulary. Similarly, dreams are more incongruous and novel than waking fantasies but would seem to draw upon a more limited stock of elements. An analogous situation arises with the schizophrenic. In his review of the literature, Maher (1972) notes the apparent contradiction between the obvious improbability and "originality" of much schizophrenic speech and the well-replicated

TABLE 8.2

Partial Correlations (Removing the Effect of Number of Words and of Sentences) between Time-in-Series and Indices of Linguistic Variability

Index	English	French
Hapax legomena percentage	.04	.00
Type–token ratio	−.04	−.09
Relative information	−.11	−.39*
Yule's K (word frequency)	−.08	.26
Yule's K (word length)	.01	.54**
Yule's K (sentence length)	.47*	.15

*$p < .05$.
**$p < .01$.

finding that it is less diverse than normal speech when assessed with indices such as the type-token ratio. Maher's own research suggests that schizophrenics have a tendency to repeat the same word in closer proximity than do normal subjects. In some ways, poetry is similar to schizophrenic speech in this respect. The same word is often repeated several times within the space of a line, as in Hugo's

Waterloo! Waterloo! Waterloo! bleak plain!

It might be argued, then, that the drive for metaphor distance or incongruity, forcing the poet towards regressive states, counteracts any tendencies toward increasing linguistic diversity which might otherwise exist.

L'EPITHETE IMPERTINENTE

A study reported by Cohen (1966) offers corroborating evidence for the prediction that poetry became more incongruous over the time covered by the French series. Cohen investigated textual samples from three poets each, from the French classical, romantic, and symbolist movements. His concept of *"épithète impertinente"* is similar to metaphor distance. It refers to the modification of a term by a predicate which is not literally appropriate—e.g., modifying an inanimate noun with an animate adjective as in Hugo's, "He mounted the bitter stairs." The frequency of such incongruous epithets was found to increase significantly from 3.6 percent for classical poetry through 23.6 percent for romantic to 46.3 percent for symbolist. Of course, all metaphors are to some degree "impertinent." Even more striking are figures which Cohen reports on clearly incongruous attribution of colors (e.g., Rimbaud's "black perfumes" or Mallarmé's "white agony"). Frequencies of such usage cannot be meaningfully computed for classical verse since there is almost no usage of color terms. However, the percentage of such usages increases from 4.3 percent in romantic poetry to 42.0 percent in symbolist poetry.

Cohen shows that increases in incongruity are not limited to the semantic level. Enjambment (punctuation in the middle of a verse) leads to a discord between pauses arising from the meaning of a poetic utterance and the metrical pauses falling at the end of each verse. A value on disruption of expectation should lead to increases in the frequency of enjambment. Cohen's figures for frequency of unpunctuated metric pauses shows that enjambment has indeed increased over time from 11 percent for classical poets through 19 percent for romantics to 39 percent for symbolists. A value on incongruity should also lead to other disruptions between sound and sense. Cohen's figures on frequency of noncategorial rhymes (rhymes between words from different grammatical categories—e.g., noun and verb rather than noun and noun) bear out this prediction: Such rhymes constitute 18.6 percent of all classical rhymes, 28.6 percent of romantic, and 30.6 percent of symbolist.

In summary, there is a clear tendency for Incongruous Juxtapositions to increase as a function of time in the French series, while there is a less strong tendency in the same direction in the English series. Further, the rate of increase in the English series is distinctly slower than in the French series. The predictions are confirmed with the exception that the relationship between Incongruous Juxtapositions and time-in-series does not reach an acceptable level of significance in the English sample. Although there is a basic linear component in the relationship between time and Incongruous Juxtapositions, Incongruous Juxtapositions does show changes in rate of increase over time. It was suggested that pressure for stylistic disintegration increases as a function of decreases in the rate of change of Incongruous Juxtapositions. Findings in regard to increases over time in, and variability of, associative meaningfulness and the results of Cohen (1966) further support the hypotheses, especially for the French series. Trends toward decreases in linguistic diversity, in the face of these increases in incongruity, seem to make sense, given the regressive origins of poetry.

Chapter 9
STYLISTIC CHANGE

The purpose of the new form is not to express
new content, but to change an old form
which has lost its aesthetic quality.

SHKLOVSKY

By *stylistic level* we mean the level at which inspirationally "given" poetic contents are elaborated or written down. If elaboration is at a level of acute consciousness, we expect an integrated, reality-oriented structure, no matter what the level of inspiration. Conversely, if elaboration occurs at a more regressed level, we expect less orientation toward purposeful communication and reality. In Chapter 3, we differentiated four ranges of style: discursive, analogical, equational, and juxtapositional. Now, texts elaborated on the analogical level ought to exhibit a higher frequency of words such as *like* and *as*, while the surrounding styles should exhibit comparatively higher frequencies of words such as *is*. The equational style does not compare, but equates; similarly, the discursive style tends not to compare elements, but to use them in descriptive phrases.

Two tags, Analogy and Being, were defined. The former contains seven words (as, like, same, seems, alike, resembles, similar). The latter contains present tense forms of the verb *to be* (is, be, are, am, being). Word-based percentages of these tags were converted to *T*-scores. Since these were related to number of sentences per document, deviation scores with the effect of number of sentences partialed out were obtained as the final

131

measures. The stylistic levels were defined in terms of the tags as follows:

1. Discursive: Being $\geq$ Analogy, with the difference being small and insignificant.
2. Analogical: Being $<$ Analogy.
3. Equational: Being $>$ Analogy.
4. Juxtapositional: Being $\doteq$ Analogy, with both occurring with low frequency.

These predictions refer to the T-score versions of the tags; in raw percentage terms, Being is always much more frequent than Analogy.

There is a possibility here for a good deal of mistagging (e.g., statements such as "he is at home" or "I like candy" are not relevant to stylistic level but would be tagged). Also, the two tags would be expected to correlate with each other because of such constructions as "is like" and "as is." But these constructions should be relatively constant across all documents. If such problems wash out the effect we are looking for, the tags will not vary over time as predicted. There is not, then, much point in enumerating and defending against them on an a priori basis.

Given the generally shallow level of eighteenth-century English verse, we expect that the stylistic shift in this case will be from the discursive to the analogical level, while the French shift should be from the analogical to the equational level. To be precise, the prediction from the theory is that in both cases stylistic shift will be from the initial level to the next lower one (in terms of less· elaboration). Of course, we cannot tell on purely theoretical grounds what level of style will be operant at any given time. When given the level of style we can, however, predict what the *next* elaborative level will be. Nor can we specify from the theory exactly *when* the stylistic changes will occur. On qualitative grounds we might expect stylistic change to occur in F6 and E6. Based on the leveling off of Incongruous Juxtapositions, we should expect pressures for stylistic change to increase after E3 and F4.

Figure 9.1 graphs changes over time of Analogy and Being for the English series. (In Figures 9.1 and 9.2 ordinates are adjusted to yield roughly comparable values. The statistical tests discussed below are based on ranks, which makes the values for the different variables exactly comparable.) In E1–E5 (see Figure 9.1) the pattern of the tags suggests a discursive style with Being marginally and insignificantly higher than Analogy. Applying the Sign test,

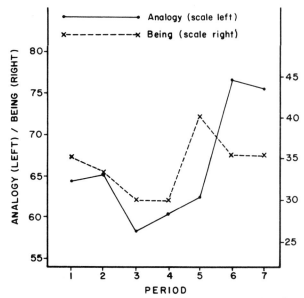

FIGURE 9.1 Mean values of Analogy and Being for the English series. Ordinates adjusted to yield comparable values.

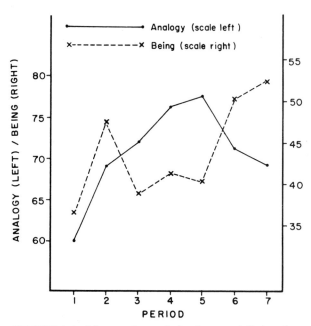

FIGURE 9.2 Mean values of Analogy and Being for the French series. Ordinates adjusted to yield comparable values.

we find $x = 6$ ($p = .40$, $N = 14$). In E6 there is a marked shift, sustained in E7, to an analogical style, with Analogy significantly higher than Being (for E6-E7, $x = 0$, $p = .03$, $N = 5$).[1] For the series as a whole, variations in Analogy as assessed by the Kruskal-Wallis one-way analysis of variance approach the .10 level ($H = 9.77$) while variations in Being are insignificant ($H = 3.43$). Analogy in E6-E7 is significantly higher than in E1-E5 (Mann-Whitney $U = 7$, $p = .001$, $n_1 = 6$, $n_2 = 15$). While Being and Analogy fluctuate over periods E1-E5, they do retain the predicted *relationship* to each other. Based on statistical evidence, it is clear that, according to our definitions, a stylistic shift occurs in E6 and is sustained in E7.

Figure 9.2 graphs changes over time of Analogy and Being for the French series. In this case our predictions are not so clearly upheld. The pattern of the tags suggests a discursive style in F1-F2, an analogical style in F3-F5 and a shift, as expected, to an equational style in F6. For the series as a whole, variations in Analogy approach the .10 level of significance ($H = 9.34$) and variations in Being are insignificant ($H = 8.56$). In F1-F2, Being is insignificantly higher than Analogy ($x = 2$, $p = .34$, $N = 6$) indicating a discursive style; in F3-F5, Analogy is significantly higher than Being ($x = 1$, $p = .04$, $N = 8$) indicating an analogical style; while in F6-F7 Being is almost significantly higher than Analogy ($x = 1$, $p = .11$, $N = 6$), indicating an equational style. Analogy decreases significantly from F4-F5 to F6-F7 ($U = 8$, $p = .07$, $n_1 = n_2 = 6$), while Being increases significantly over the same period ($U = 6$, $p = .03$, $n_1 = n_2 = 6$).

The prediction of a shift from analogical to equational style is upheld, but we are faced with two patterns which were not expected. First, the pattern of the tags assigns a discursive style to F1 and F2. Second, Analogy is not constant over periods F1-F5. The sequence of styles—discursive to analogical to equational—is as predicted by the theory. However, as will be seen in the next chapter, F3 does not behave as we would expect a period of style change to (i.e., level of regression does not decrease). We seem to be confronted with "stylistic slippage." This aspect of the course nineteenth-century poetry was discussed in Chapter 5. The tags are picking up a real phenomenon: French romantic poetry tends to be much more rhetorical and discursive than does its English counterpart; the poets of F3 explicitly rebel against this and begin a "purification" of poetry. However, there is a gradual *slippage*

---

[1] The reduced N results from tied ranks.

toward lesser degrees of elaboration rather than a clearcut stylistic change of the sort evident in E6 and F6. This does not change the fact that there is a definite shift away from analogical style in F6. Just as stylistic slippage did not prevent the need for a cubist revolution in painting, it did not do so in poetry.

The notion of stylistic slippage would explain why Analogy increases continually from F1 through F5. It is probable that, over this period of time, the autonomy of French poetry (as measured by, e.g., sales figures) increased continually. Thus, the theory would support such an hypothesis. We cannot, however, embrace the idea of stylistic slippage too hastily. It will be seen in the next section that, for the French series, Analogy follows the fluctuations of the regression indices rather closely. Therefore it could be argued that Analogy is really measuring regression rather than elaboration. In summary, then, there is good evidence for a stylistic shift in F6, but stylistic variations are not as simple or as independent of level of regression as was predicted for the French series.

Several recent studies complement our findings concerning the stylistic change in the English series. Wright (1974) presents figures concerning the usage of the progressive as opposed to the simple present tense in English verse. He notes that in English, as opposed to many other European languages, the progressive present tense has gradually displaced the simple for the denotation of concrete actions in the present. Thus, we tend to say "I am walking in the garden" rather than "I walk in the garden" to describe a present action. The simple present is used to express more general or habitual states and in conditional phrases; in other words, it is used in more abstract contexts. Within the framework of our stylistic levels, its usage would, then, be appropriate to more discursive, secondary process levels of elaboration. From another perspective, of course, it could be seen as more formal or less colloquial than the progressive tense. Wright counted frequency of usage of the progressive tense in 326,000 lines of verse, some of it from the periods covered by our English series. His figures indicate a fairly clear stylistic break beginning in period E5 and completed by E6. The five poets in periods E1 to E4 for whom he gives figures use the progressive tense in an average of .05 percent (SD = .07) of their lines. The range is from no usage at all for Collins to .16 percent for Gray. On the other hand, the eight poets in periods E5 to E7 use the progressive in .71 percent (SD = .28) of their lines, almost a fourteenfold increase. The range is from Blake's .18 percent to Shelley's 1.12 percent. Applying the

Mann–Whitney U test to the difference between E1–E4 and E5–E7 usages, we obtain $U = 0$ ($p = .001$, $n_1 = 5$, $n_2 = 8$). The change is a fairly discontinuous one, with no overlap in the two distributions. Only period E5 gives evidence of transition, with Blake being closer to the old style and Burns' rate of .85 percent clearly adhering to the new style. Presumably, Wright's figures indicate a stylistic break in E5, while ours indicate one in E6 because the indices tap different aspects or levels of the same process. Perhaps increased usage of the progressive tense is a "leading indicator," or a more sensitive index, of the stylistic disintegration that our tags hypothetically measure.

We have argued that stylistic elaboration is maintained by need or desire for communication. Increases in the autonomy of the poet lessen this need and thus allow stylistic disintegration. One possible index of orientation toward communication would be the addressee of the lyric poem. Hankiss (1972) has tabulated changes over time in the person or entity addressed by English lyric poetry. His major categories included human beings, magical or abstract entities, and nobody. To the extent that the poet loses his orientation toward communication with an audience, he should direct his poems to no one in particular. Hankiss counted the addressees of 1,223 English poems, some from periods overlapping ours. In this sample, 21 percent of poems written by poets born between 1630 and 1715 (partially overlapping periods E1 to E3) were addressed to nobody. The corresponding figure is 19 percent for poets born between 1715 and 1765 (overlapping periods E3 to E5). The percentage rises to 26 percent for poets born between 1765 and 1800 (overlapping periods E5 to E7) and to 31 percent for those born between 1800 and 1825. Incidentally, the percentage continues to rise fairly regularly until it reaches 67 percent for poets born after 1925. For our purposes, the crucial point is that the upward inflection in the curve occurs at a point consistent with what would be predicted from changes in the other stylistic indices.

During what roughly corresponds to period E5, Miles (1957) found the addition and dropping of large numbers of words in the poetic lexicon to form the so-called romantic vocabulary. This shows up clearly in her tabulations of most frequently used words in this period, as compared with previous periods. It would seem that the poets of this period attempted to change the *subject* of discourse and some of its surface characteristics rather than its fundamental *structure*. Similar efforts were made in France during period F5, but representatives of it do not turn up in our samples. Such changes in poetic subject matter are apparently common precursors of stylistic change in the sense that we have used the term. This is consistent with the notion that poetic structure is more rigid and less susceptible to change than is poetic content.

Chapter 10
REGRESSION

Au fond de l'Inconnu pour trouver du nouveau.
BAUDELAIRE

The first step in the construction of the content-analytic measures of regression was to derive from the theoretical and empirical literature on regression and primitive thought a number of explicit characteristics of primary and secondary process thinking. Those indicators that seemed likely to be reflected in the content of texts were selected for further development. Of course, many aspects of such thought do not exhibit themselves in a manner that would be picked up from simple word counts. For example, the illogicality of primitive thought manifests itself, not in any specific set of words, but in the way words are combined. The basic assumption behind the regression categories is that different contents are "indigenous" to different levels of regression or states of consciousness; that, e.g., one is not likely to load his communications with references to sensations unless these dominate the state of consciousness from which he writes. The main objection that can be made to this is that such contents can also be due to artifice or to the specific subject matter being considered. This is certainly true in regard to any one of the tags, but in order to obtain a high regression score, it is necessary to exhibit high values on more than one or two tags. If one were to argue that it is at times stylish to use the whole constellation of regressive words, it becomes a legitimate question to ask why just this set of words should be so valued. Of course, autobiographical writings by poets support the contention that poetry tends to be written in altered states of consciousness and that its basic content is seldom completely the result of logical artifice.

MEASURES

The rationale and form of the regression categories is the same as Holt's (1968) coding scheme for measuring regression in the service of the ego on the Rorschach, and Pine's (1960) for measuring it on the Thematic Apperception Test. It is also similar in some respects to the coding scheme used by Kalin, McClelland and Kahn (1965) for measuring *n* Sentience. The categories (along with the rationale underlying each), component tags, and five most frequently occurring words in each are as follows:

Secondary Process: Included as an inverse indicator of regression. The tags tap the cognitive, behavioral, and modulating, or controlling, aspects of secondary process cognition.

1. Abstraction: know, may, thought, why, think.
2. Social Behavior: say, tell, call, speak, meet.
3. Instrumental Behavior: make, find, work, toil, build.
4. Restraint: must, stop, bind, reign, guard.
5. Order: simple, measure, array, balance, divide.
6. Temporal References: when, now, then, time, old.
7. Moral Imperatives: should, right, virtue, hono(u)r, law.

Emotion: Theoretically, emotions are drive derivatives, or modulated and rarified drives. Affect should, then, indicate a mild regression from pure secondary process thought.

1. Positive Emotion: smile, joy, rest, happy, delight.
2. Anxiety: fear, tremble, dread, terror, blush.
3. Sadness: tear, sad, pain, weep, woe.
4. Love: love, friend, dear, kind, pity.
5. Aggression: break, war, beat, strike, wound.
6. Expressive Behavior: cry, sing, art, play, sigh.
7. Glory: gold, great, pride, divine, glory.

Defensive Symbolization: The tags in this category tap disinhibition or lack of control, modulation, and focus; in most of the tags, however, this is reflected in a "projection" of these attributes onto the extrapsychic world.

1. Passivity: (death, dead, die), lie, bed, slow, calm.
2. Voyage: wander, desert, beyond, search, ship.

3. Random Movement: wave, roll, spread, swell, shake.
4. Diffusion: shade, shadow, cloud, fade, veil.
5. Chaos: wild, crowd, ruin, chance, confuse.
6. Parataxic/Integrative ratio: and/but, which, if, though, thus.

Sensation: Dominance of sensations and perceptions as opposed to abstractions or emotions ought to indicate a further increment of regression.

1. General Sensation: fair, charm, beauty, beautiful, lovely.
2. Touch: touch, thick, stroke, smooth, rough.
3. Taste: sweet, taste, bitter, sweetness, savor.
4. Odor: breath, perfume, scent, nose, smell.
5. Sound: hear, voice, sound, listen, ear.
6. Vision: see, light, look, shine, green.
7. Cold: cold, winter, snow, freeze, cool.
8. Hard: rock, stone, hard, glass, iron.
9. Soft: soft, gentle, tender, murmur, whisper.

Drives: Drive imagery is one of the principle psychoanalytic indices of regression.

1. Oral: breast, drink, lip, mouth, tongue.
2. Anal: sweat, rot, dirty, disgust, filth.
3. Sex: lover, kiss, naked, caress, Venus.

Icarian Imagery: According to Ogilvie (1968), this type of imagery refers to primitive, preverbal symbolization of drives and affects. As such, it should be related to Silberer's (1912) autosymbolic phenomena: use of images, rather than words, as the units of cognition.

1. Ascend: hope, rise, fly, throw, flight.
2. Height: up, sky, high, tree, grow.
3. Descend: fall, drop, sink, descend, plunge.
4. Depth: down, deep, beneath, under, low.
5. Fire: sun, fire, flame, burn, warm.
6. Water: sea, water, stream, flow, shore.

Regressive Cognition: Most of the tags in this category tap, in straightforward form, attributes of deeply regressive cognition and states of consciousness.

1. Unknown: secret, strange, unknown, mystery, void.
2. Timelessness: eternal, forever, immortal, eternity, endless.

3. Consciousness Alteration: dream, sleep, (a)wake, fancy, mad.
4. Brink-Passage: road, wall, door, steps, path.
5. Narcissism (body parts): eye, heart, hand, face, head.
6. Concreteness (spatial references): at, where, over, out, long.

Several summary variables were constructed from various combinations of the categories. Primary Process was conceived as a direct indicator of degree of regression. It is composed of the weighted sum of Sensation, Icarian Imagery, Defensive Symbolization, Regressive Cognition and Drives. Emotion and Secondary Process are not included, since they theoretically indicate slight and inverse regression, respectively. It will be remembered that tags were converted to T-scores with mean of 50 and standard deviation of 10 in order to weight them equally in arriving at category sums. Since there are differing numbers of tags in the categories, the means of the categories differ. In order to give each category equal weight, each was divided by the number of tags comprising it before obtaining the Primary Process sum. This procedure gives category scores with equal means and roughly equivalent standard deviations. Thus:

$$Primary\ Process = S/9 + II/6 + RC/6 + DS/6 + D/3$$

where S = Sensation, etc. This leads to a mean of 250 (SD = 22.16) across all forty-two poets for Primary Process.

Primary Process is not weighted to represent the relative "depth" of regression to which the component tags refer. There are theoretical reasons for assuming that, for example, a high frequency of Regressive Cognition indicates deeper regression than a high frequency of Sensation. The use of factor scores gives us measures which are so weighted. Such scores were derived from the factor analysis carried out on the correlation matrix generated by the forty-four tags listed above plus eight other theoretically related tags. For all factor scores the total mean is 0 (SD = 1).

VALIDITY

It might be well to provide some evidence which suggests that the various categories do indeed measure regression. Theoretically we would expect regressive imagery to be connected with the exhibition of symptoms of psychopathology (cf. Fenichel, 1945; Werner, 1948). Correlations between ratings of presence or absence of such symptoms in the poets in our samples and degree of regressive imagery in their poetry are given in Table 10.1. The method of rating is described in Martindale (1972a). The correlations provide a striking validation of the scoring system for the French poets; for the English, Secondary Process seems to be the best (inverse) measure of regression. The low correlations between pathology and Emotion in both samples justifies our interpretation of Emotion as a relatively nonregressive category lying conceptually between Secondary Process and Primary Process. Emotion apparently measures a slight or shallow mode of regression that is, in general, readily accessible to both normal and pathological personality types.

The dictionary has also worked, as would be predicted from several theoretical perspectives in studies of a variety of other texts. More primary process and less secondary process imagery have been found in folktales of primitive as opposed to more complex preliterate societies (Martindale, 1973c) and in fantasy stories of creative as opposed to uncreative subjects (Hines and Martindale, 1973a). These findings are consonant with the primitive mentality hypotheses of writers such as Lévy-Bruhl (1910) and the regression in the service of the ego hypothesis of Kris (1952), respectively. In research aimed at testing

TABLE 10.1

Biserial Correlations between Psychopathology and the Regression Categories

Category	Sample		
	English (N = 20)	French (N = 20)	Total (N = 40)
Primary Process	.46*	.85***	.53***
Secondary Process	−.62**	−.76***	−.55***
Emotion	−.04	−.15	−.02
Sensation	.13	.50**	.30*
Drive	−.05	.57**	.23
Defensive Symbolization	.06	.54**	.29*
Regressive Cognition	.43*	.60**	.29*
Icarian Imagery	−.06	.71***	.32*

*p < .10.
**p < .05.
***p < .01.

psychoanalytic hypotheses (cf. Fenichel, 1945), more primary
process and less secondary process imagery were found to occur in
psychoanalytic sessions devoted to "work" than in those manifest-
ing patient resistance and defensiveness (Martindale, Reynes, and
Dahl, 1974). The same pattern occurred in sentences containing
verbal tics, as opposed to those containing no tics, in a study of a
patient suffering from Gilles de la Tourette's syndrome (Martindale and Hines, 1973b). Presumably, a momentary lowering of
niveau mentale allows the tics to emerge and is marked by
increased primary process content. Similarly, letters of schizophrenics were found to contain less secondary process and
insignificantly more primary process words than control letters
(Martindale, unpublished). In research deriving from the arousal
theory of states of consciousness, correlations have been found
between EEG alpha activity and frequency of secondary process
content in speech (Hines and Martindale, 1973a); further, unpublished research has shown that increments in arousal produced by
white noise produce decrements in such content.

Finally, research into the symbolic meaning of literary voyages
to heaven and hell and of alchemical parables has produced results
consonant with the hypotheses of Jung (1959) and others.
Martindale (1973b) tested the notion that Dante's *Inferno*
symbolizes a "descent into the unconscious" or regression
followed by a return to normal consciousness in the *Purgatorio*
and a second, more cognitive, regression symbolized by the
journey to heaven depicted in the *Paradiso*. Indeed, primary
process content was found to increase across the cantos of the
Inferno and *Paradiso* and to decrease across the first two-thirds of
the *Purgatorio*. Later research has disclosed analogous trends in
the visit to hell described in Book 6 of the *Aeneid* and in the
alchemical "journey" described in *Aurora consurgens* (von Franz,
1966).

In the context of our questions regarding validity, the method
of factor analysis can be of help in seeing whether the set of
interrelationships among categories is as it is theoretically expected to be. The correlation matrix analyzed was generated by all
of the Primary Process, Secondary Process, and Emotion tags as
well as by the following, hypothetically related, tags: PMR-MT,
PFR-FT, PFR-MT, PMR-FT (measures of appropriate and of
cross-sexual role descriptions; see Chapter 12), Icarus Sequence
(Ascend occurs before Descend in a sentence), Persephone
Sequence (Descend occurs before Ascend in a sentence), Diabolic,
and Angelic. Thus, a 52 × 52 correlation matrix (with $N = 42$) was

factored. No rotation of the six obtained factors was done, since the unrotated factors presented a clear picture. The first two factors accounted for 19.6 and 12.2 percent of total variance, respectively. The remaining ones accounted for small amounts of variance, and their content suggested that they were of a residual nature. Table 10.2 presents loadings of the tags on the first two factors.

Factors I and II seem to be getting at different aspects of regression. The first factor involves a polarity between abstraction and control versus concrete symbolization (Icarian Imagery), sensations, and other hypothetical attributes of primary process thought. Thus, it seems to represent the more cognitive aspects of regression. Factor II involves most prominently a continuum ranging from Drives to Emotions. In terms of the psychoanalytic view of emotion as differentiated or sublimated drive, this factor makes sense as one involving directness of drive expression.

It is of help to examine what Kassebaum, Couch, and Slater (1959) have termed *fusion factors* (the factor spaces defined by variables which are about equally highly loaded on two factors, e.g., tags which load highly on both Factors I and II), since an interesting pattern emerges when the four fusion sectors are examined along with the four pure factor sectors. Figure 10.1 shows how the tags arrange themselves in these eight sectors and provides tentative labels for the factors and fusion factors. If we examine the diagram with our major categories in mind, we see that they tend to arrange themselves in a counterclockwise pattern roughly in order of increasing regression. The positive pole of Factor I (sector I+) seems to be differentiated from sector I+II− by the quality of affectiveness. The three tags in sector I+ are relatively abstract, while those in sector I+II− refer to secondary process contents and operations closer to the level of experience. Two—Moral Imperatives and Restraint—involve connotations of duty, which may be seen as a refined level of affect. Temporal References would seem to be closely dependent upon lived experience (cf. Bergson's concept of *temps vécu*). Positive Emotion is clearly on the affective level. Its presence in this sector, however, is consistent with the phenomenological relationship of joy and elation with higher levels of consciousness. Sector II− defines the emotional end of the factor we have seen as dealing with the directness of drive expression. Besides a few Sensation tags, sector I−II− contains most of the Defensive Symbolization tags. It seems to describe words associated with a slight degree of regression. With Sector I− we move to the tags associated with Icarian Imagery as well as the remaining Sensation tags. It is

TABLE 10.2

Factor Loadings of Tags with Loadings of Greater than ±.20

Factor I	Loading	Factor II	Loading
		PMR–FT	.63
		Anal	.59
		Brink-Passage	.49
		Oral	.47
		Narcissism	.42
		Sex	.33
Social Behavior	.77	Hard	.31
Abstraction	.75	Timelessness	.29
Moral Imperatives	.70	Concreteness	.28
Instrumental Behavior	.66	Consciousness Alteration	.27
Restraint	.50	Persephone Sequence	.25
Temporal References	.30	Fire	.24
Positive Emotion	.22	PFR–MT	.23
PMR–MT	−.26	Restraint	−.20
Sound	−.30	Moral Imperatives	−.20
Brink-Passage	−.30	Passivity	−.22
Diabolic	−.30	Vision	−.28
Sex	−.31	Taste	−.28
Timelessness	−.33	Aggression	−.32
Chaos	−.35	Voyage	−.32
Voyage	−.36	Sadness	−.37
Random Movement	−.39	Parataxic/Integrative	−.39
PFR–FT	−.40	Love	−.40
Expressive Behavior	−.40	Time	−.42
Touch	−.40	Sound	−.42
Hard	−.40	Ascend	−.46
Parataxic/Integrative	−.43	Chaos	−.50
Descend	−.47	Soft	−.51
Odor	−.48	Expressive Behavior	−.52
Cold	−.48	Anxiety	−.55
Soft	−.48	Random Movement	−.56
Ascend	−.49	Glory	−.60
Passivity	−.50	General Sensation	−.65
Concreteness	−.50	Positive Emotion	−.66
Sadness	−.52		
Unknown	−.55		
Angelic	−.57		
Height	−.57		
Consciousness Alteration	−.59		
Depth	−.61		
Fire	−.61		
Narcissism	−.62		
Vision	−.65		
Water	−.69		
Diffusion	−.71		

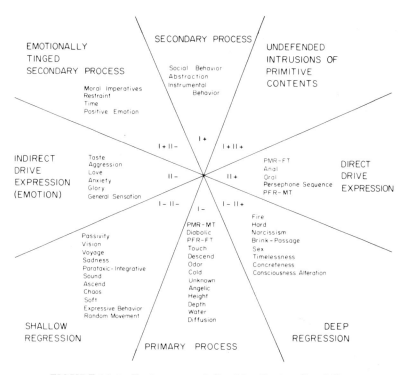

EMOTIONALLY
TINGED
SECONDARY PROCESS

SECONDARY PROCESS

UNDEFENDED
INTRUSIONS OF
PRIMITIVE
CONTENTS

Social Behavior
Abstraction
Instrumental
Behavior

Moral Imperatives
Restraint
Time
Positive Emotion

INDIRECT
DRIVE
EXPRESSION
(EMOTION)

Taste
Aggression
Love
Anxiety
Glory
General Sensation

I + II −   I +   I + II +

II −   II +

PMR−FT
Anal
Oral
Persephone Sequence
PFR−MT

DIRECT
DRIVE
EXPRESSION

I − II −   I −   I − II +

Passivity
Vision
Voyage
Sadness
Parataxic-Integrative
Sound
Ascend
Chaos
Soft
Expressive Behavior
Random Movement

PMR−MT
Diabolic
PFR−FT
Touch
Descend
Odor
Cold
Unknown
Angelic
Height
Depth
Water
Diffusion

Fire
Hard
Narcissism
Brink-Passage
Sex
Timelessness
Concreteness
Consciousness Alteration

SHALLOW
REGRESSION

PRIMARY PROCESS

DEEP
REGRESSION

FIGURE 10.1   Factor space defined by Factors I and II.

interesting to note that Vision and Sound occupy sector I−II−
while Touch and Odor occupy sector I−. Touch and Odor are less
abstract and closer to the level of raw experience (Arieti, 1967)
than Vision and Sound. Aside from the exception of Taste, the
counterclockwise sequence of sense modalities supports the
hypothesis that such movement through the sectors from I+
describes a course of greater and greater regression. The presence
of Icarian Imagery in this sector is consistent with Ogilvie's (1968)
hypothesis that it represents a primitive symbolization of mental
contents. Sector I−II+ contains most of the Regressive Cognition
tags. Sector II+ contains the two most primitive drive tags, Oral
and Anal, and the two cross-sexual imagery tags, PMR−FT (use of
feminine themes in sentences referring to males) and PFR−MT (use
of masculine themes in references to females). This clustering
conforms with both Freudian and Jungian notions of deep
regression. It differs from the other sectors in that most of its
contents are subject to active suppression and repression due to
their taboo nature. Sector I+II+ is, not surprisingly, empty. It
would not seem to be a contentual one: from its position, it seems

to represent a sort of thought that is not actually regressed in the usual sense, but that does not repress taboo regressive contents and, perhaps, mechanisms. As such, none of the tags in the dictionary is geared toward picking it up. The cognition characterizing this sector probably finds its nearest analogy in the low elaboration–shallow regression sequence discussed in Chapter 3.

This analysis of the first two factors, accounting together for almost one-third of the variance of the regression tags, provides further evidence that the categories do indeed possess an acceptable degree of construct validity. The factor space described conforms with what would be expected from the theoretical and empirical literature on regression. This, and the fact that the factor analysis was carried out on representatively selected texts, reinforces the belief that the factors are real ones, that a radically different factor structure would not emerge with another sample of similar poetic texts.

Factor analyses have been done based on a variety of other types of texts which suggest a good deal of stability for the first factor. The first factors emerging from these factor analyses, based on the seven major *categories* rather than on tags, are given in Table 10.3, along with the results of a comparable analysis of the present data. As may be seen, a similar first factor accounting for about 30 percent of the variance emerges in almost all of these studies. With one exception, it shows high positive loadings on Regressive Cognition and Icarian Imagery and a high negative loading on Secondary Process. This is the same first factor that emerged in the analysis of tag intercorrelations. Some of the categories do fluctuate in their factor loadings as a function of type of text. Thus, in texts marked by heavy colloquial usages of words in the Sensation category (e.g., "I see the point," "get in touch"), this category malfunctions. The second, or drive versus emotion, factor has proved much less stable. Something resembling it at times emerges, but more often it is "collapsed" into the first factor as in Reynes' (1974) analyses of speech in psychoanalytic sessions.

SUMMARY VARIABLES

In regard to changes over time, increases in depth of regression until the periods of stylistic change are predicted. During these periods, regression should decrease significantly. For the French sample, stylistic change was found to begin in period F6. Our

TABLE 10.3

Unrotated First Factor Loadings of the Regressive Imagery Categories in Several Samples

Sample	N	Regressive Cognition	Icarian Imagery	Sensation	Drive	Defensive Symbolization	Emotion	Secondary Process	Percent of variance
1. Poetry (present sample)	42	.67	.84	.66	.18	.73	.09	−.78	43.6
2. *Inferno*	34	.92	.33	.51	.36	.13	−.43	−.56	32.1
3. *Purgatorio*	33	.73	.65	1.03	−.06	−.03	−.46	−.57	39.5
4. *Paradiso*	33	.71	.59	.37	.09	−.01	.52	−.71	31.8
5. Folktales	45	.46	.82	.28	.41	−.61	−.23	−.66	28.4
6. Schizophrenic and nonschizophrenic letters	109	.46	.61	−.37	.54	.31	.38	−.55	22.2
7. Thematic Apperception Test stories: Harvard University Ss	23	.60	.52	−.71	.42	.35	.43	−.72	30.8
8. Thematic Apperception Test stories: University of Maine Ss	72	.80	.36	.55	−.11	.01	−.46	−.62	24.0
9. Psychoanalytic patients	9	.05	.72	.67	.98	.91	−.54	.21	45.6
10. Psychoanalytic therapists	9	1.01	.64	.60	.71	.10	−.65	−.44	45.1
$\overline{X}$	41	.64	.61	.36	.35	.19	−.14	−.54	34.3

Note. 2, 3, 4 from Martindale (1973b); 5 from Martindale (1973c); 6, 7, 8 from Martindale, (unpublished); 9, 10 from Reynes (1974).

measures indicate the same for the English series, although it will be recalled that data obtained from other investigations suggest that stylistic change may have begun in period E5. Thus, increasing regression through period 4 or 5, a decrease in period 6, and a possible increase in period 7 are predicted for both series.

Once a new style is established, the theory predicts that regressive imagery will begin to increase again. There is no theoretical reason to assume that stylistic change will consume exactly one twenty-year period, that regressive imagery will begin to increase in period 7 rather than in a later unsampled period. Due to the greater autonomy of the French series, regression is expected to reach deeper levels before the period of stylistic change.

Primary Process

Figure 10.2 presents information on changes in Primary Process content across periods. Variation for the French series is significant ($H = 10.27$, $p < .10$). Primary Process imagery increases to a peak in F5 and, after this, decreases in F6 and F7. Stylistic change evidently continues in F7, rather than being completed in F6. The increase from F1 to F5 is significant ($U = 0$, $p = .05$, $n_1 = n_2 = 3$), as is the decrease from F5 to F6 ($U = 1$, $p = .10$, $n_1 = n_2 = 3$). The French series reaches deeper levels of regression than does the English. If we compare F4 with E4, we obtain $U = 0$ ($p = .05$, $n_1 = n_2 = 3$).

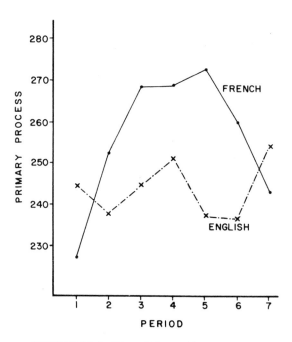

FIGURE 10.2   Mean Primary Process scores.

The variations in Primary Process are not significant for the English series (H = 3.25). Nonetheless, the pattern is as expected, except that the peak of the first regressive cycle is reached in E4 rather than in E5. If one examines the pattern of mean *ranks* per period, there is an increase from E1 to E2 rather than the decrease seen with the T-scores; the extreme secondary process bias of John Byrom tends to distort the values of all of the regression indices for E2. For the English series, the only relevant significant difference is that for the increase from E6 to E7 (U = 0, p = .05; n_1 = n_2 = 3). There is a fairly consistent reason why, in this and other cases, the English series approximates the expected pattern but falls short of significant variation: Byrom in E2, Smart in E3, and Cowper in E4 produce scores that are vastly disparate from those of the other poets in each of these periods. Where the other poets tend to produce poetry consistent with theoretical expectations, the three poets in question generally do not. For example, the ranks of the poets from E2 through E4 on Primary Process—ranks run from 1 (least amount of Primary Process) to 21 (largest amount of Primary Process)—are as follows:

Poet	Rank
Byrom	1
Thomson	19
Dyer	18
Gray	17
Collins	16
Smart	2
Cowper	3
Beattie	20
Mickle	21

In this case, the order of means is not disturbed, but the outlying scores prevent significance tests from reaching acceptable levels. Byrom, Smart, and Cowper consistently produce such aberrant scores. Although there are reasons why they do not follow theoretical predictions, they do not justify their exclusion. However, because of these poets, we have tended to place more faith in the patterns of variation in the English series than might seem warranted by many of the significance test results.

Byrom produced a few poems of very high quality and thus assured himself of a place in anthologies. However, the majority of his poetic output consists essentially of rhymed letters to friends. This is what constitutes most of our sample. In writing these productions, Byrom probably did not consider himself to be writing poetry per se. Variation in the English series is further clouded by the tendency of two of these poets to write "ahead of their time." There is a fairly clear increase in regression for the series: E1(Watts, Gay, Pope)-E2(Thomson, Dyer)-E3(Gray, Collins)-E4(Beattie, Mickle), followed by a decline in E5 and E6. However, Smart in E3 and Cowper in E4 seem to anticipate the poets of E5 and E6 in content and style. Blake in E5 and Coleridge in E6, on the other hand, anticipate on many counts the E7 poets. Thus, we seem to have a series of poets that does behave roughly as expected, along with a smaller "fast series" that produces content that coheres not with their own but with succeeding periods. Significantly, the "fast series" contains two definitely psychotic poets (Cowper and Smart) and a third who was probably psychotic (Blake). It might be argued that this led to functional increments in their autonomy from the audience and access to regressive states over those enjoyed by their contemporaries.

Factor Scores

Let us turn to the factor analytic measures of regression. Factor I (secondary process versus primary process) follows closely the pattern of Primary Process (see Figure 10.3). Peaks occur in E4 and E7 and in F5. Kruskal-Wallis analyses of variance yield $H = 4.57$ (*ns*) for the English series and $H = 9.37$ ($p \rightarrow .10$) for the French. On Factor I the French series reaches greater depths of regression, but this is less clear-cut than before (for E3-E4 versus F4-F5, $U = 10$, $p = .12$, $n_1 = n_2 = 6$). Movement from E1-E2 to E3-E4 approaches significance ($U = 10$, $p = .12$, $n_1 = n_2 = 6$), but the decline from E3-E4 to E5 and E6 fails to reach an acceptable level of significance. However, the increase from E5-E6 to E7 is significant ($U = 3$, $p = .08$, $n_1 = 3$, $n_2 = 6$). For the French series, F1 and F7 are both significantly lower than F5 on Factor I scores ($U = 0$, $p = .05$, for F1 versus F5 and $U = 1$, $p = .10$, for F5 versus F7; in both cases, $n_1 = n_2 = 3$).

Factor II (directness of drive expression) exhibits no meaningful pattern in the English case ($H = 4.92$, *ns*). However, as may be seen in Figure 10.4, it follows the expected regression curve in the French series: there are increases through F5, a decrease in F6, and an increase in F7. Here, $H = 15.51$ ($p < .01$). The increase from F1 to F5 is significant ($U = 0$, $p = .05$, $n_1 = n_2 = 3$). The decrease in Factor II scores from F5 to F6 and the increase from

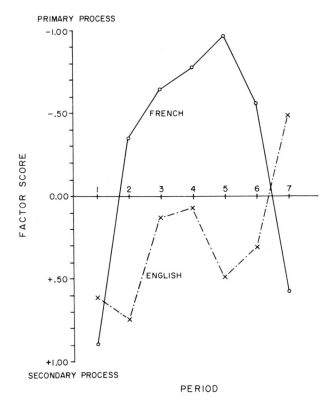

PRIMARY PROCESS

SECONDARY PROCESS

PERIOD

FIGURE 10.3 Mean scores on Factor I (Primary Process versus Secondary Process).

F6 to F7 are both significant (in both cases, $U = 1$, $p = .10$, $n_1 = n_2 = 3$).

The increase of Factor II in F7 makes somewhat equivocal the answer to whether this period marks the beginning of a new regressive cycle or continues the stylistic shift begun in F6, as suggested by results for Primary Process and Factor I. The probable answer is that breakdowns in elaboration due to stylistic disintegration are accompanied by analogous breakdowns in "sublimation" of drives, as represented by Factor II. In this interpretation, the decrease in Primary Process words in F7 indicates that movement is toward *less* elaboration and *less* regression. This is to say, F7 represents a continuation of the stylistic change or breakdown in level of elaboration begun in F6, but this breakdown in elaboration is so extreme as to be functionally equivalent to movement to a deeper level of regression. The increase in Secondary Process words in F7

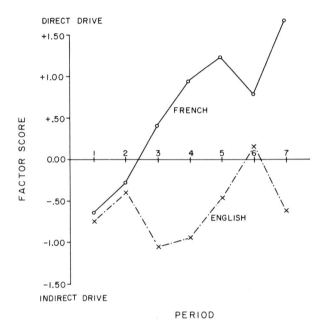

FIGURE 10.4   Mean scores on Factor II (Direct versus
Indirect Drive Expression).

connotes not secondary process cognition but rather use of
secondary process elements in somewhat the same way an acute
schizophrenic makes use of abstract words that are apprehended in
a concrete manner. Such an explanation is consonant with our
theoretical interpretation of the regression and elaboration dimensions and is supported by an examination of the movement of the
French series in the factor space defined by Factors I and II (see
Figure 10.5). The presence of F7 in the margin of sector I+II+
(undefended intrusions of primary process content), which we
defined in terms similar to those used in this explanation, supports
this argument.

   The general movement of the French series in Figure 10.5 is in
a counterclockwise direction from Sector I+II− (affectively based
secondary process) through II− (emotion or sublimated drive
representation), I−II− (shallow regression), I− (primary process),
I−II+ (deep regression), and II+ (direct drive representation)
toward I+II+ (undefended intrusions of primary process content).
This is precisely the course of increasing net regression as defined
in the discussion of the factor space. Movement in this space of
the English series is more limited but also shows a trend toward
regression: the net movement is from Sector I+II− to Sector I−II−:

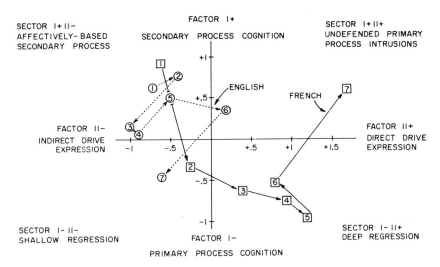

FACTOR I+

SECTOR I+ II−
AFFECTIVELY-BASED
SECONDARY PROCESS

SECONDARY PROCESS COGNITION

SECTOR I+ II+
UNDEFENDED PRIMARY
PROCESS INTRUSIONS

FACTOR II−
INDIRECT DRIVE
EXPRESSION

FACTOR II+
DIRECT DRIVE
EXPRESSION

SECTOR I− II−
SHALLOW REGRESSION

FACTOR I−

SECTOR I− II+
DEEP REGRESSION

PRIMARY PROCESS COGNITION

FIGURE 10.5 Movement of the French and English series in the factor space generated by Factors I and II.

i.e., from affectively based secondary process cognition to shallow regression. As predicted, change in the English series is analogous to that in the French in that both move in the direction of greater regression, but the English series moves at a shallower level. In each case, the periods of stylistic change exhibit a reversion back toward the secondary process pole, allowed presumably by the forging of a new, less elaborated stylistic structure, which leads to a decrease in the amount of regression required to produce a given degree of novelty.

REGRESSION CATEGORIES

There should, in regressive phases, be a tendency for the regressive categories to reach peaks or plateaus in an order consonant with the theoretical and empirical depths of regression that they measure: Secondary Process, Emotion, Defensive Symbolization, Drives and Sensation, and Icarian Imagery and Regressive Cognition. After peaks are reached there should be some tendency for the categories to decrease in frequency as significantly deeper levels of regression are reached. The English series should exhibit a working out of this pattern on a less regressed level than the French. That is, Secondary Process and Emotion should be prominent in their variation while the remaining regressive categories, if they vary meaningfully at all, should reach peaks lower than those seen in the French series.

Figure 10.6 presents graphs of mean ranks per period on each of the categories for the French series. Variations in Emotion are significant at the .01 level ($H = 14.80$), while those in Regressive Cognition are significant at the .05 level ($H = 14.33$). Variations in Secondary Process, Sensation, and Icarian Imagery are significant at the .10 level ($H = 10.34$, 10.66, and 9.88 respectively), but changes in Defensive Symbolization and Drive fail to reach statistical significance. With the exception of Icarian Imagery, the French sample provides excellent confirmation of the prediction. The categories reach peaks as defined by mean ranks in the following order: Secondary Process and Emotion in F1, Defensive Symbolization in F2, Sensation in F3, Drives in F4, and Regressive Cognition in F5. While Icarian Imagery reaches a peak in F2, it

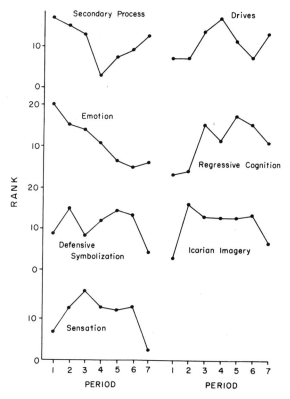

FIGURE 10.6 Mean ranks of French periods on the regression categories.

remains at a high level throughout the regressive cycle. The other categories decline more sharply after reaching peaks. Icarian Imagery seems to operate as a sort of all-or-none indicator of medium and deep regression, as it differs insignificantly in periods F2 through F6 but occurs with very low frequency in F1 and F7. While it correlates negatively with Secondary Process, it does not differentiate among the gradations of regression proper, at least in this context.

The pattern of peaks of the categories supports the notion that we are dealing with a series of texts written at successively deeper levels of regression. Emotion decreases strikingly throughout the series. That it does not increase in F5 and F6 with Secondary Process raises a problem. We should expect Emotion to increase before, rather than after, Secondary Process. Its failure to do so suggests the persistence of the explicit sanctions against emotional rhetoric which appeared with the reaction against romanticism in F3. These seem to have exhibited an autonomy of their own. However, Emotion does re-emerge, albeit in a displaced position, in F7. The importance of the theme of love for Apollinaire and Eluard supports the hypothesis that emotion does indeed assume increased importance in F6 and F7.

The quantitative findings fit well with the qualitative investigation of the French series carried out in Chapter 5. We find F1, the "classical" period, characterized by abstract and emotional concerns. In period F2, the first generation romantics (Lamartine, Hugo, Nerval), both of these fall off in frequency while Defensive Symbolization and emphasis on Sensation increase. Icarian Imagery increases sharply, reflecting, in part, activism opposed to the more classic stasis of F1 and, perhaps, a sort of defensive reaction to the lure of regressive passivity. It is significant that the use of emotional words decreases from F1 to F2. This suggests that the emotionality that later poets reacted against in the romantics was already on the wane in the romantic period itself. Of course, F1 is as justly called preromantic as classic; the density of emotional words is not surprising in that period.

With period F3 we see further decreases in Emotion and Secondary Process, along with increases in Sensation, Drives, and Regressive Cognition. Thus, the period of Baudelaire, Musset, and Gautier seems, by our measures, to constitute a rather straightforward extension of the voyage toward regression begun by the romantics in F2, rather than, as some qualitative observers have suggested, a reaction against romanticism. There may have been reaction, but not on the basic level that our measures tap.

The same might be said of F4 (Mallarmé, Corbière, Verlaine). Emotion continues to decline and the usage of Secondary Process words drops precipitously. Drive imagery reaches a peak, replacing sensational dominance. Thus, F4 represents the lowest ebb of Secondary Process and the greatest saturation of texts with Drive imagery. Sensation, Regressive Cognition, and Icarian Imagery are also at high levels. On all of these counts F4 seems to be the most clearly regressive French period.

Period F5 presents a more opaque picture. Verhaeren provides the poetry exhibiting the deepest level of regression in our sample. Laforgue, on the other hand, anticipates the stylistic shifts of F6 and F7. Rimbaud occupies an intermediate position, showing both deep regression and some tendency toward innovation on the stylistic level. In F5 emotional words continue to disappear, but Secondary Process shows an increase and Drives decrease—both of these mainly because of Laforgue. Regressive Cognition, however, reaches a peak. This is consonant with the deeply regressed symbolist poetry of this generation.

Period F6, a clear stylistic turning point on qualitative grounds, exhibits declines in Drives, Defensive Symbolization, Regressive Cognition, and Emotion, along with further increases in Secondary Process. This suggests a rising to shallower levels of regression. This tendency is exacerbated in F7, the surrealist period: Defensive Symbolization and Sensation reach absolute low points for the French series; Icarian Imagery and Regressive Cognition drop sharply while Secondary Process continues to increase. However, references to drives increase definitely in frequency. It would seem that, while regression does decrease, elaboration decreases sharply as well, permitting the breakthrough of primitive mental contents.

Figure 10.7 graphs mean ranks per period on each of the categories for the English series. On the basis of correlations with poets' psychopathology, Secondary Process was seen to be the best index of regression for the English series. And, indeed, it is the only category exhibiting significant variation ($H = 9.88$, $p <$ .10). The pattern of Secondary Process suggests the culmination of the first regressive cycle in E3 and the beginning of a second cycle in E6. However, most of the rise in Secondary Process in E4 is due to Cowper. On other counts, E4 does seem to represent the culmination of the first regressive cycle. The pattern of variation in Defensive Symbolization and Regressive Cognition (based on reranked sum of ranks—see Figure 10.7) supports this notion; however, changes in this score fail to reach statistical significance.

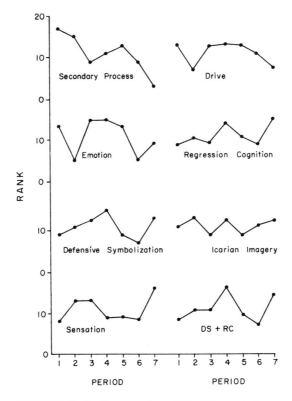

FIGURE 10.7 Mean ranks of English periods on the regression categories.

Sensation, Emotion, and Drive also vary roughly but insignificantly according to predictions.

CONCRETENESS

One hypothetical aspect of the secondary process–primary process continuum is the abstract–concrete dimension. According to Goldstein (1939) what we have called regressive thought is concrete while secondary process thinking is characterized by abstraction. Degree of regression should be inversely related to degree of abstraction, which should be directly indexed by the abstractness of vocabulary. Paivio, Yuille, and Madigan (1968) asked subjects to rate 925 nouns on a seven-point abstract-concrete scale. The resulting norms were taken as a dictionary for use with SEMIS and applied to the textual samples. The output was, for each document, the mean concreteness of the words in that document that were found in the dictionary.

As expected, concreteness correlated with indices obtained from the Regressive Imagery Dictionary. For the English sample, it correlates .24 (*ns*) and −.47 ($p < .05$) with Primary Process and Secondary Process, respectively. For the French sample, the corresponding values are .61 ($p < .01$) and −.66 ($p < .01$). Changes in concreteness over time are graphed in Figure 10.8. Because of large intraperiod variability, Kruskal–Wallis analyses of variance fail to reach significant levels. But there are clear trends over time in both series. The correlation between time-in-series and concreteness is .51 ($p < .01$) for the English series and .53 ($p < .01$) for the French. For the French series, the increase from period F1 to F6 is significant ($U = 0$, $p = .05$, $n_1 = n_2 = 3$). The increases from the first period to both F4 and F5 are also significant at the same level. The decrease from F6 to F7 is not significant. The rise from period E1 to the first peak in the English series is not significant, nor is the dip in E6, but the increase from E6 to E7 is ($U = 0$, $p = .05$, $n_1 = n_2 = 3$). As may be seen in the figure, the trends parallel those found with the regression indices. The major divergence is

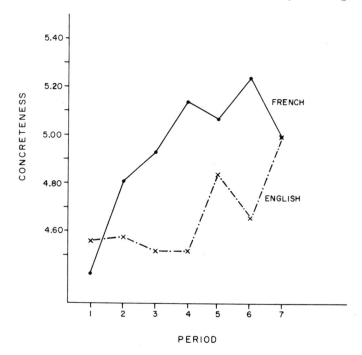

FIGURE 10.8 Mean concreteness values.

the high value for period F6. where concreteness should be decreasing rather than increasing. A similar pattern was noted for Icarian Imagery, and perhaps a similar explanation will suffice. That is, perhaps concreteness acts as an index of medium and deep regression, but is insensitive to gradations. Another more likely possibility would be that the stylistic change of period F6 involves an increased outward orientation, which brings with it a more concrete vocabulary. Rather than writing about *chimeras* and *eternities*, the F6 poets write of *airplanes* and *chairs*. Thus, their vocabulary is more concrete than that of the F4 and F5 poets, but this indicates less, rather than more, regression. At any rate, the convergence of results using two different measuring instruments— the Regressive Imagery Dictionary and Paivio, Yuille and Madigan's concreteness norms—measuring regression with different words and different techniques is encouraging.

Chapter 11
THE MOVEMENT OF POETRY
IN SEMANTIC SPACE

What whirlwinds of ordure I see on the horizon.
HUYSMANS

A factor analysis was carried out on an intercorrelation matrix generated by all eighty-four original nonoverlapping tags and co-occurrence scores in the Regressive Imagery Dictionary. An orthogonal fixed rotation (Couch, 1967) performed on the resultant factors yielded a new factor structure of considerable interest. Three factors were rotated through the semantic differential tags to conform the factor space to Osgood, Suci, and Tannenbaum's (1957) semantic space. The first factor was rotated to maximize the positive factor loading of Strong and the negative loading of Weak. Similar strategies were followed with Good and Bad, and with Activity and Passivity. The three rotated factors, indicated as F_p, F_e, and F_a (for Potency, Evaluation, and Activity), accounted for the following percentages of total variance:

Factor	Variance
F_p	8.43%
F_e	7.99
F_a	6.09
	22.51%

163

Since neither French nor English periods varied significantly on F_a, it will not be discussed further. In terms of the tags which load highly on it (see Table 11.1), F_p has strong overtones of masculinity versus femininity, while F_e has connotations of the social versus asocial dimension. Thus, there is a tendency toward concretization and specification of the factors, which is altogether

TABLE 11.1

Factor Loadings of the Tags on the First Two Semantic Differential Factors (Factor Loadings above .30 Are Given)

F_p		F_e	
Tag	Loading	Tag	Loading
		Good–Bad Juxtaposition	.49
		Moral Imperatives	.47
		Icarus Sequence	.46
		Abstraction	.44
		Aspiration	.40
Strong	.60	Novelty	.40
Male Role	.60	Integrative	.38
Positive Emotion	.60	Time	.36
Instrumental Behavior	.52	Restraint	.35
Glory	.52	Related Others	.35
Aggression	.48	Paradise	.33
Moral Imperatives	.40	Adornment	.33
General Sensation	.38	Social Behavior	.33
Anxiety	.36	Strong	.30
Random Movement	.31	Weak	.30
Cold	−.31	Expressive Behavior	−.31
Narcissism	−.32	Odor	−.32
Integrative	−.32	Unknown	−.32
Fire	−.33	Anal	−.34
Passivity	−.35	Narcissism	−.36
Self	−.37	Trivial	−.36
Consciousness Alteration	−.37	Touch	−.38
Concreteness	−.37	Flowers	−.39
Weak	−.37	Hard	−.40
Icarus Sequence	−.38	Sound	−.42
Water	−.38	Female Role	−.45
Flowers	−.38	Cold	−.45
Height	−.40	Hard	−.45
Unknown	−.41	Diabolic	−.45
Diffusion	−.43	Oral	−.49
Transmute	−.50	Angelic	−.54
PMR-FT	−.52	Sex	−.61
Analogy	−.68		

consistent with the poetic approach to communication. When the tags are looked at in terms of the semantic differential factors, they seem to pick up "projective" aspects of regression. The positive poles of F_p and F_e recall Jung's concept of Spirit, or *Logos*—the masculine, secondary process, conscious principle. The negative poles of F_p and F_e recall his concept of *Eros*, which governs the "unconscious," with tags bearing connotations of evil, darkness, and femininity showing high loadings. Thus, Female Role loads negatively on the evaluation factor and PMR-FT (use of female themes in sentences dealing with males) loads negatively on the potency factor. One could, then, "locate" *Logos* (or secondary process cognition) in sector F_p+F_e+ and *Eros* (or primary process cognition) in sector F_p-F_e-. That the semantic differential tags themselves, with the exception of Strong, do not load very highly on their own factors makes this symbolic interpretation more plausible.

In both samples, there are significant decreases over time on F_p. For the English series, $H = 12.65$ ($p < .05$); for the French series, $H = 10.65$ ($p < .10$). As may be seen in Figure 11.1, movement is from potent, masculine connotations toward weak, effeminate ones. Movement on F_e is also significant for both

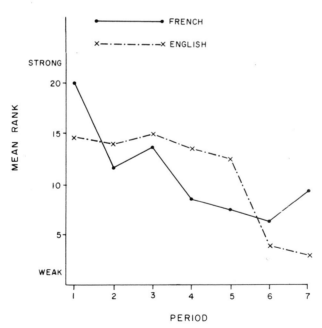

FIGURE 11.1 Mean ranks of F_p scores.

samples: $H = 11.87$ ($p < .05$) for the English series and $H = 14.23$
($p < .05$) for the French series. The trend is curvilinear in both
cases, with a tendency toward prosocial, good connotations at the
beginnings and ends of the series and asocial, evil ones in the
middle periods (see Figure 11.2). Movement of F_e parallels that on
degree of regression.

A clear picture emerges when we examine the positions of the
two samples in the factor space set up by F_p and F_e (see Figure
11.3). The English series begins in E1 with verse characterized by
prosocial masculinity and assertion. Movement in the first few
periods is away from the strong, good sector toward the strong,
evil sector (but only *to* a neutral position) and then, gradually,
there is a slippage away from potency toward connotations of
weakness. Probably, such purely eighteenth-century forms as the
early Gothic novel and the creations of the Marquis de Sade
represent an extrapolation of the movement seen from E1 to E3,
but without the slippage toward weak and impotent connotations.
Such a continuation was barred to the more socially controlled
verse of the century. With E6, there is a leap back toward
connotations of goodness and down toward connotations of

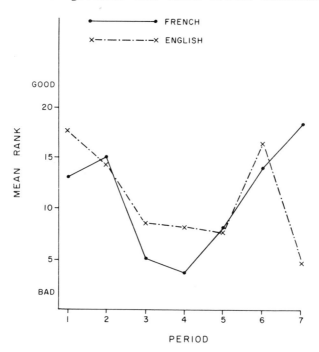

FIGURE 11.2 Mean ranks of F_e scores.

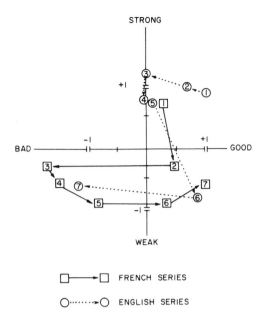

FIGURE 11.3 Mean factor scores for each
period in the factor space generated by F_p
and F_e.

effeminate weakness and passivity. The sector occupied by E6
seems to characterize well early romanticism, with its passive but
definitely outward-oriented and prosocial stance. E7 represents
the beginning of the movement toward late romantic decadence
and lasciviousness.

Period F1 occupies a point virtually identical with that of E5;
movement from F1 to F3 parallels that of E5 to E7. During this
era, the French periods move with the English periods of twenty
years earlier, but tend to outstrip them on the evaluative dimension.
This parallelism makes sense in terms of what we know concerning
the diffusion of poetic form and content from England to France
during this era. Periods F4 and F5 show a slippage toward a more
impotent stance at still rather extreme levels of asociality.

Interestingly, F6 and F7 occupy the sector occupied by F2
and E6, the early romantic periods. It is to be noted that these
four periods occupying sector F_p-F_e+ are all in some sense
periods of stylistic shifts. It is reasonable that they should be
socially oriented, given the negative relationship between regression and such an orientation: stylistic change allows decreases in
the degree of regression. That these periods produced verse bearing

connotations of impotence and effeminacy reflects the fact that the movement back toward secondary process cognition (which we located in sector $F_p + F_e +$) accompanying stylistic shifts in modern times is only relative and not extreme enough to bring about movement back to the egoistic, assertive attitude characterizing early eighteenth-century verse.

If, as we have argued, the rotated semantic differential factors pick up "projected" and connotational attributes of regressive cognition, as opposed to being direct indices of such cognition, this would explain why variation on the factor scores is significant for the English series where variation on the more straightforward measures of regression was insignificant.

Chapter 12

SEXUAL ROLE POLARITY IN MODERN FRENCH POETRY

Art has created a supernatural being, the Androgyne,
beside which Venus disappears.

PELADAN

According to Neumann (1954, p. 315), "consciousness and the ego always experience themselves as masculine," while regressive states are experienced as feminine. Bachelard (1960) similarly comments on the *"ivresses de femme"* of deep reveries. Kris (1952) holds that inspiration tends to be "fantasized" in terms of feminine, passive receptivity, while Jung (1959), Levey (1940), and Sharpe (1930) argue that it is automatically symbolized as a reunion with the mother. According to Jung, the unconscious is often symbolized by feminine (anima) figures while the ego or conscious mind is symbolized by male (animus, hero) figures. Thus, there have been many contentions that regression is associated with a feminine feeling tone. Given that the creative process entails regression, it follows (Neumann, 1954, p. 355) that "creativity in all its forms is always the product of a meeting between the masculine world of ego consciousness and the feminine world of the soul." Cocteau[1] argues a similar point:

---

[1] Quoted by Shroder, 1961, p. 233.

169

> Art is born of the coitus between the masculine element and the feminine element of which we are all composed, in finer balance in the artist than in other men. The result is a sort of incest, a union of one's self with one's self, a parthenogenesis.

The way in which this union is symbolized varies as a function of degree of regression. Neumann (1954) describes the form of this symbolization in the successive states of ego development. Deep regression is symbolized by the submission of a weak, androgynous hero to a "Great Mother" figure symbolizing the unconscious. Her characteristics are undifferentiated: She is "terrible and devouring, beneficient and creative; a helper, but also alluring and destructive; a maddening enchantress, yet a bringer of wisdom; bestial and divine, voluptuous harlot and inviolable virgin, immemorially old and eternally young" (Neumann, 1954, p. 322). Myths such as those of Hyacinthus and Narcissus, where the hero submits passively and impotently, as well as those concerning Attis, Pentheus, and Hippolytus, where the hero struggles futilely, represent this state. At this level, there is confusion of sexual roles, and even some tendency toward reversal, with males being depicted as weak and passive and females as strong and dominant. Lesser and more manageable degrees of regression are symbolized by myths where a powerful hero such as Hercules descends into the underworld in order to slay a dragon or other evil figure and to rescue a captive anima figure usually associated with gold or some other treasure. Dragon and maiden represent negative and positive aspects of the unconscious, respectively. Here, male and female figures are well differentiated.

Given these considerations, if level of regression varies historically in artistic creation, so should presentation of sexual roles. In Chapter 4, we derived Praz' (1933) "descriptive law" concerning the course of cross-sexual imagery in nineteenth-century literature from our theory of literary change. In this chapter, we provide quantitative evidence that, in our sample of twenty-one French poets, cross-sexual imagery does indeed behave in accord with Praz' empirical and our theoretical law.

The investigation of male and female roles is not central to the content-analytic study, but represents a corollary exercise. There are two difficulties involved. First, the connection between cross-sexual imagery and regression is more tentative than, say, the association of oral imagery with regression. Second, while cross-sexual imagery is theoretically related to regression, it cannot be used as a regression index, because it is structurally a subtype of metaphor distance. Like metaphor distance, it involves the juxtaposition of incongruous elements. Phenomenologically, there is a clear differentiation. Being based upon Osgood's semantic differential axes, the polarities involved in Incongruous Juxtapositions are theoretically all-inclusive: if one is to make any sort of juxtaposition, it must accrue to one of these dimensions, just as, if one is to move, he must move within the three spatial dimensions. Cross-sexual imagery is, in large measure, a subset of Strong–Weak juxtapositions, but one that it hardly seems likely would be used without a basis in personal motivation. It would be hard to argue that Péladan, for example, wrote his endless *Décadence latine*, with the androgyne an omnipresent emblem, merely in a disinterested attempt at achieving novel or incongruous images. Because of the many other ways of achieving originality, some explanation beyond mere need for novelty would seem necessary for such an idiosyncratic form of incongruity.

The general procedure was to examine the occurrence within sentences containing references *only* to male figures or *only* to female figures of themes usually seen as masculine or feminine. Thus, the analysis was carried out on a subset of sentences from the total sample of poetry: Pure Male Role (PMR) units and Pure Female Role (PFR) units. These sentences were selected automatically by the computer by reference either to the editing marks (/M and /F) described in Chapter 7 or to the dictionary tags Male Role and Female Role. These tags contain every proper name occurring in the sample, as well as all other identifying words (e.g., he, she, knight). Because of the time-consuming nature of the editing required, this analysis was carried out only for the French series.

A number of tags compose the categories Male Theme (MT) and Female Theme (FT). Many of these were also used in the Primary and Secondary Process categories. Since the final scores are based on co-occurrences, with basal frequencies statistically removed, changes in these frequencies do not spuriously determine them. The tags were selected by means of a hand-scored pretest using themes that were expected to differentiate male and female role presentations. The tags selected for the present study had, in the pretest, significantly differentieated PMR and PFR units in poetic texts where it was theoretically expected that these units should contain proper sexual themes. These texts were early eighteenth-century English ones, different than the ones used in the present study. In the pretest, these themes in the aggregate showed a convergence over the course of time until they did not differentiate PMR and PFR units in a sample of late nineteenth-century English poets; however, such convergence was *not* a basis for selection or rejection of a tag.

Male and Female Theme tags are listed here along with the five most frequently occurring words in each:

Male themes

1. Diabolic: black, dark, fate, curse, hell.
2. Fire: sun, fire, flame, burn, warm.
3. Strong: god, could, king, power, father.
4. Hard: rock, stone, hard, glass, iron.
5. Abstraction: know, may, thought, why, think.
6. Instrumental Behavior: make, find, work, toil, build.

Female themes

1. Angelic: white, pure, pale, sacred, angel.
2. Flowers: flower, garden, bloom, blossom, roses.
3. Weak: child, little, lose, poor, cannot.
4. Sadness: tears, sad, pain, weep, woe.
5. Soft: soft, gentle, tender, murmur, whisper.
6. Social Behavior: say, tell, call, speak, meet.
7. Synthesis: hold, together, join, while, melt.

Four co-occurrence scores eventuate from the occurrence of Male Themes (MT) and Female Themes (FT) in PMR and PFR sentences: PMR–MT, PFR–FT, PMR–FT, and PFR–MT. PMR–FT and PFR–MT should index cross-sexual role presentations: PMR–FT gives a measure of frequency of usage of female themes in sentences referring to male figures, while PFR–MT indicates use of male themes in sentences concerning females. On the other hand, PMR–MT is a measure of co-occurrence of male themes with male roles and PFR–FT of co-occurrence of female themes with female roles. Percentages based upon sentence counts rather than upon word counts are appropriate in this case. Each of these, in percentage form, was divided by the appropriate expected percentage score for each document (e.g., PMR $\cap$ MT/PMR $\times$ MT) to yield an index independent of the frequency of occurrence of the component tags. When any of the four scores are referred to, it is this corrected form that is meant.

The frequency of cross-sexual imagery should follow the hypothesized frequency of regressive imagery: That is, PMR–FT and PFR–MT should increase from F1 through F5, decrease in F6, and possibly increase again in F7. The changes in PMR–FT and PFR–MT are illustrated graphically in Figure 12.1. It is apparent that the prediction is strikingly confirmed for PMR–FT, while PFR–MT follows a similar pattern but reaches a peak in F4. The

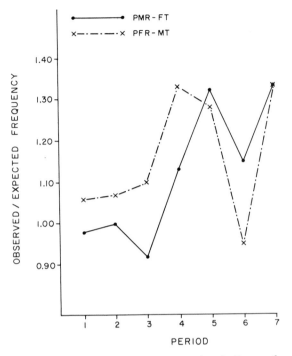

FIGURE 12.1 Mean scores on the indices of cross-sexual imagery.

overall variations of PMR–FT and PFR–MT are both significant at the .05 level ($H = 14.00$ and 11.30, respectively). PMR–FT increases significantly from F1 to F5 ($U = 0, p = .05, n_1 = n_2 = 3$). The decrease from F5 to F6 reaches the .10 level ($U = 1, n_1 = n_2 = 3$), but the increase from F6 to F7 is insignificant ($U = 2, p = .20, n_1 = n_2 = 3$). For PFR–MT, the increase from F1 to F4 ($U = 0, p = .05, n_1 = n_2 = 3$), the decrease from F4 to F6 ($U = 0, p = .05, n_1 = n_2 = 3$), and the increase from F6 to F7 ($U = 1, p = .10, n_1 = n_2 = 3$) are all significant. The changes in the presentation of sexual roles over time seems to entail the *addition* of cross-sexual references rather than significant decrements in appropriate sexual references, since neither PMR–MT nor PFR–FT vary significantly over time ($H = 4.45$ and 2.82 respectively).

It must be noted that PFR–MT reaches a clear peak in F4 while PMR–FT does not peak until F5. The peaking in F5 is in closer conformity with theoretical expectations. Two possible causes suggest themselves. First, since our subjects are males, PFR–MT is a less direct expression of cross-sexual concerns; hence, it is less distressful, easier to allow into consciousness, and could therefore be expected to emerge first. Second, from a Jungian perspective, hermaphroditic references (which we could expect to base themselves upon the male role and to show up in PMR–FT) represent a more primitive level than imagery involving cruel, diabolic, and powerful female figures: at the deepest levels of regression, there is a *unio mystica* involving the merging of male and female principles and a concomitant falling-off of feminine dominance.

It might be argued that appropriate role–theme combinations should decrease and inappropriate ones increase for our hypothesis to be clearly substantiated. PMR–MT does show a trend in this direction, but PFR–FT does not; indeed, it reaches its highest level in F5, where cross-sexual imagery is also maximal. The reason may lie in the peculiar treatment of women in poetry in general. Chapter 11 showed that Female Role loads highly on the *negative* pole of the evaluation factor. In particular, the reason may lie in the mode of presentation of the cruel woman. Take Swinburne's Dolores:

Cold eyelids that hide like a jewel
Hard eyes that grow soft for an hour.

The fatal woman is alternately nurturant and cruel. The two aspects intertwine and reverberate.

Inappropriate role–theme combinations show a rise in period F7 following consistent and significant dips in F6. This dip and rise was also seen in Drives and Factor II (direct drive expression) scores. It is possible to explain the pattern of sexual incongruity) with the same device used to explain the pattern found with drive imagery: a lowering of elaboration and defense which allows normally taboo regressive contents into consciousness. Of course, since sex role incongruity is at least logically a form of Incongruous Juxtapositions, we cannot be sure that the increase in sexual incongruity in F7 is not artificial, is not based upon a conscious striving for novelty. Remarks like Breton's "I wish I could change my sex like I change my shirt" point to cross-sexual concerns in F7; however, the more prevalent attitude in this period was one of explicit attachment to heterosexuality, thus suggesting that at least part of the increases in sexual incongruity in this period may merely reflect attempts to increase metaphor distance.

Regardless of the explanation of these changes, the results would seem to offer a compelling, albeit indirect, case for the independence of changes in poetic content from changes in the larger society. It would be very difficult to make a case for the argument that sex roles did *in fact* change in the directions suggested by poetic content across the nineteenth century. If anything, an opposite movement might be argued. We tend to think of regency males as rather more effete than Victorian gentlemen. Similarly, early nineteenth-century women's fashions emphasized a flat-chested look while being more sexually provocative and revealing than later fashions. Even if it were granted that males became more feminine and females more masculine across the course of the nineteenth century, we would then have to postulate that this trend reversed itself around 1900 and then resumed around 1920. The changes in poetic content do not seem to reflect directly or even to mirror in an inverted fashion any changes in actual sex roles for which a plausible case could be made.

The results offer striking confirmation of Praz' (1933) qualitative findings for the nineteenth century. That incongruous role-theme images are thoroughly diffused throughout our random samples (were they not, large variance would prevent significant statistical results), rather than occurring only in patches, supports the view that this is an important variable to be considered in the analysis of poetic texts. Our findings in regard to the incidence of cross-sexual imagery in the nineteenth century provide an excellent example of the power of a quantitative approach. Praz (1936) has himself commented on the content analytic method in his review of Spurgeon (1935), where he claimed that an elaborate content analysis was hardly necessary for the admittedly rather nonspecific inferences and conclusions that Spurgeon made. But the point is not so much *what* we conclude but, rather, what we conclude *from*: The fourteen points in Figure 12.1 are not, of course, as fascinating as the nearly five hundred pages which Praz takes to document his case, but they are a good deal more convincing. Where Praz allows himself to pick his examples from all of European literature, both prose and poetry, and where he often seems forced to go to obscure and forgotten authors to prove a point, we have limited our selection of texts to a principle beyond our control. One has the suspicion that a scholar of Praz' erudition could have, with only a little more effort, selected a series of examples to prove an opposite thesis. We can be relatively confident that a second random sample would yield roughly the same results. Where Praz is free to decide anew with each example what constitutes cross-sexual imagery, we are committed to a single, explicit set of criteria. Where, quantitatively, he is limited to *more* and *less*, we are able to expand this and to state approximately how much "more" or "less." Finally, the probability of Praz' assertions is indefinite; we are able to say that the probability of our conclusions is about 20 to 1 in favor of correctness.

Chapter 13
METAPHOR DISTANCE AND REGRESSIVE IMAGERY AS DETERMINANTS OF EMINENCE

A master of any art avoids excess and defect but seeks the intermediate.

ARISTOTLE

Eminence constitutes a sort of second-order dependent variable. Although it accrues to a given poet, it is as much a function of audience attitudes as of verse content. As such, it is relevant in testing predictions concerning the relationship between audience esteem and regressive content. We ranked the eminence of each author according to the number of pages assigned him in the Oxford anthologies. Since different volumes were used, there were three noncomparable ranges of eminence: that for French poets, that for eighteenth-century English poets, and that for nineteenth-century English poets. The last group was too small for meaningful statistical evaluation and was hence disregarded in analyses of eminence.

It is hypothesized that eminence is most readily assigned to periods of medium regression and metaphor distance, and that eminence is less readily granted to poets producing texts with extreme metaphor distance than to those producing texts with comparably extreme degrees of regressive imagery. The prediction is based upon the model of audience acceptance of poetic communications, which is, in turn, based on Berlyne's (1971) hypothesis concerning the inverted-U relationship between pleasure and arousal potential. The audience goes to poetry with the expectation of some novelty, but this is counteracted by the general tendency toward negative affect when confronted with stimuli exhibiting a too-strong arousal potential. In accordance with the discussion in Chapter 3, it is reasonable, however, to assume greater withdrawal in the face of the incomprehensible than of the distasteful.

Figure 13.1 presents the total number of pages assigned to the three poets in each period. Numbers for E6 and E7 were omitted from statistical analysis because they are derived from a different anthology than the bulk of the English eminence figures. For the English series, a Kruskal–Wallis analysis of variance on the

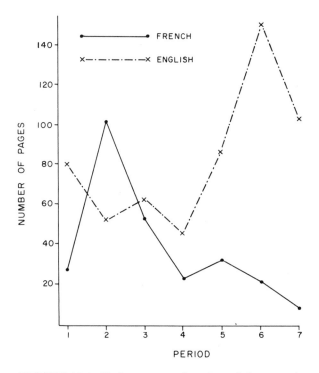

FIGURE 13.1 Eminence as a function of time: total number of pages assigned to the poets in each period. (Total for F2 is based on Vigny rather than Nerval.)

interperiod variation of the truncated E1–E5 series yields $H = 2.63$ (*ns*); for the French series, however, $H = 14.25$ ($p < .05$). Examination of Figure 13.1 indicates that both eminence curves are curvilinear. First, propinquity in time to the assigner of eminence seems to account for much of the variance in the French series; however, it cannot account for all of it, since the curve is not linear. In the English series, leaving aside E6 and E7 for a moment, it is seen that eminence is highest in E1 and E5. It is low in E3 and E4, which are periods of comparatively deep regression and extreme metaphor distance, and in E2, where regression and metaphor distance tend to be even *less* evident than in E1 and E5. Thus, in this case, high eminence seems to be assigned to periods exhibiting medium metaphor distance and regression. The peak of eminence in F2 suggests the same for the French series. Periods E6 and E7, were they to be compared with *later* English periods, would undoubtedly also be periods of medium regression and metaphor distance.

The correlations in Table 13.1 support these speculations. We see that, in the English series, eminence is correlated positively with Secondary Process and negatively with Primary Process. When Primary Process is broken down into its component categories, the extremeness of the negative correlations is in proportion to the depth of regression that the categories measure. The correlations with Emotion and Sensation are scarcely different from zero, while correlations with categories measuring deeper

TABLE 13.1

Correlations between Eminence (number of pages)
and the Major Variables

Variable	English[a] ($N = 15$)	French[b] ($N = 21$)
Primary Process	−.36	.05
Secondary Process	.27	.13
Emotion	−.12	.32*
Sensation	−.10	.26
Defensive Symbolization	−.22	.04
Regressive Cognition	−.50**	−.16
Drive	−.25	−.10
Icarian Imagery	−.25	.17
Incongruous Juxtapositions	.07	−.35*

[a]Includes all poets in E1–E5.
[b]Includes Nerval, rather than Vigny.
*$p < .10$.
**$p < .05$.

levels of regression range from −.25 for Drives and Icarian
Imagery to −.50 for Regressive Cognition. In the French series,
where the baseline of regression is deeper, eminence correlates
most highly with Emotion and Sensation, both indices of medium
regression. Significantly, the correlation with Secondary Process is
positive, but only half as large; presumably, this is because
"medium regression" implies a deeper level of regression in the
French series than in the English. In the French sample, eminence
is negatively related with only Drives and Regressive Cognition,
which tap deep levels of regression. The relationship between
eminence and Incongruous Juxtapositions is equivocal. There is no
relationship in the English sample. However, for the French series,
eminence is somewhat more negatively related to Incongruous
Juxtapositions than to regressive imagery, as expected.

We have rather solid evidence in support of the hypothesis
drawn from the theory. The importance of this is far-reaching, for
it allows us to build a sort of conversion or correction "equation"
by which the regression theory of artistic change can be related to
qualitative cyclical theories of artistic change. These theories of
growth, flowering, and decay—all based upon qualitative evalua-
tions, or eminence—postulate cycles which should be out of phase
with, but related to, the objective cycles of regression described in
the present study. There is no objective reason for speaking of
periods of decay and decadence, except in regard to the state of
mind of artists, since in our framework such periods represent
peaks or furthest extensions of styles, rather than declines. That is,
they seem to be periods where the artist surpasses his audience's
tolerance for regression and metaphor distance, rather than
periods where he sinks below his audience. A period of flowering,
on the other hand, represents in our transformation a period of
quantitative mediocrity, a period which produces works of art that
large numbers of critics and people in general enjoy.

Theories based on qualitative grounds have no stable zero-
points; these depend upon the theorist's adaptation level in regard
to metaphor distance and regression; this in turn depends on his
position in time and his personality. Taking this into account, it
should be possible to cull some of the insights of such cyclic
theories and attach them to our more stable cycles of regression:
where they speak of excellence, we would probably find medium-
range quantitative values; there they speak of mediocrity or
badness, we would probably find either very high or very low
quantitative values.

Chapter 14

THE EFFECT OF EXTERNAL CONDITIONS ON POETRY

Literature is the noise of the wheels of history.
LESLIE STEPHEN

This chapter describes the results of analyses performed to assess the effect of external, or extrapoetic, factors on the major textual variables. The theoretical question to be answered regards the relative weight of external, as opposed to internal (i.e., within the poet or the poetic subculture), factors. Adequate data on external conditions are at hand only for the English series, so all reported analyses deal only with that series. Since this is a low autonomy group, we may expect it to provide a stringent test of the relative weight of internal versus external forces. It should be noted, however, that the findings reported here should be regarded as tentative until they have been cross-validated in other unrelated poetic samples. Five external variables, all derived from Sorokin's (1937) study of social change, were investigated. Two tap external social conditions, while three tap external cultural conditions.

The major procedural question was how to collate the external variables with the textual ones. First, the question of whether prior-period, contemporary-period or even posterior-period external variables ought to be investigated is not altogether obvious. Second, deciding what to take as contemporary is not a straightforward task. Our periods are defined in terms of

181

birthdates, thus preceding the timespans when the poets were actually writing. In regard to the first problem, we decided to explore prior-, contemporary-, and posterior-period relationships; however, only relations between contemporary external variables are reported here, since they tend to yield the highest relationships between external and textual variables. Where Sorokin's data could be broken down into yearly figures, contemporary external events were defined as those occurring between fifteen and thirty-four years of age of each poet. For the poets in our sample for whom information is readily available, only Blake had composed less than half (as defined by our random samples) of his verse by age thirty-five. For others, the percentage was much higher. In cases where Sorokin's data could not be broken down into yearly figures, poets' birth periods were the basis for divisions of the external variables. In these cases, the literary periods were taken as beginning and ending thirty years after the corresponding birth periods. For example, E1 contains poets born between 1670 and 1689 and is assumed to correspond to a period of production between 1700 and 1719. This method yields results which are skewed in relation to the first method, with the direction of skewness depending upon whether a poet was born toward the beginning or the end of a period. This cannot be helped, since the method is forced upon us by the form of Sorokin's tables. Other methods would have required so much interpolation as to yield meaningless data.

The construction of each variable is described below. The social variables were based upon tables in Sorokin (1937) which give yearly figures for England; they were collated with each poet's lifespan according to the first method outlined. The cultural variables were derived from tables which give figures only for twenty- or twenty-five-year periods; the second method of collation was used in these cases. Whenever interpolation was necessary (e.g., where our periods included only part of an event, or where it was necessary to get twenty-year figures from twenty-five-year tables), an assumption of uniform distribution across time was made. The measures are

1. External social stress: Total casualties (killed and wounded) in wars during the period, divided by the population of England (in the year nearest to the midpoint of the period for which information was available) to give total casualties per 1000 of population. The source for casualties was Sorokin (1937, Vol. III, "Appendix to Part Two"). Population figures were obtained from

Mitchell and Deane (1962). Sorokin's figures are estimates based on a number of sources.

2. Internal social stress: The sum of Sorokin's measures of intensity of internal disturbances during the twenty-year period. These measures are geometric means derived from ratings from 1-100 on several dimensions: the social area involved, duration, intensity, and number of participants. For detailed criteria see Sorokin (1937, Vol. III, pp. 393-396).

3. Dominant philosophical emphasis: Three steps were involved in Sorokin's determination of philosophical emphasis for a period. First, all recorded philosophical thinkers were listed. Second, each was assigned a weighting corresponding to his importance as defined by objective factors such as the number of monographs devoted to him. Third, each was assigned as a partisan of idealism or materialism. The measures adopted are percentages of total weighted sums for each of these variables. They are not mirror images because of Sorokin's use of a mixed category. Only figures for Europe as a whole are given. (Rating methods are described in Sorokin, 1937, Vol. II, p. 14 ff; data were extracted from Table 14, p. 187.) The polar categories are defined as follows (p. 183):

a. Idealism is "a system which maintains that the ultimate or true reality is spiritual, in the sense of God, of Platonic ideas, of spirit, of soul, or of psychic reality."

b. Materialism "holds that the ultimate reality is matter, and that spiritual or immaterial phenomena are but a manifestation of it, are simply the result of the motion of particles of matter."

4. Dominant moral emphasis: Sorokin's method in obtaining these ratings was the same as that used in obtaining the indices of philosophical emphasis: they are based upon the same philosophers and weightings but, of course, pertain to the system of ethics espoused. Our source is Sorokin (1937, Vol. II, Table 29, p. 488). The polar categories are defined as follows (pp. 481-483):

a. Ethics of principles express a belief in principles emanating from God or some other absolute source and a denial that increases in happiness should be a primary goal.

b. Ethics of happiness "regard sensate happiness as the supreme value and make everything else a means for its achievement and quantitative increase." In addition, it is relativistic and regards rules as man-made.

5. Technological change: Defined as the absolute number of scientific discoveries (in mathematics, astronomy, biology, medicine, chemistry, physics, and geology) and technological inventions for each period in England. The source is Sorokin (1937, Vol. II, Table 9, p. 150). Numbers are approximate, since linear interpolation was used to estimate the needed figures from Sorokin's twenty-five-year sums.

Two internal variables were investigated. Time-in-series (rank from 1 to 21 based upon birth date) is used as an index of need for novelty. Later poets should experience greater pressures toward novelty than earlier ones. A second internal variable, psychopathology, refers to a characteristic of the poets rather than of the poetic subculture. Ratings of presence or absence of psychopathological symptoms were obtained from life history data. Martindale (1972a) describes the procedure for obtaining these ratings.

DEGREE OF RELATIONSHIP

The theory gives recognition to the importance of external conditions; however, rather than dealing directly with them, it attempts to specify their degree of influence according to certain structural parameters. There is no a priori reason to predict that internal variables should show higher correlations with the textual variables than should external variables in this particular case. However, if this pattern is found, it would provide powerful support for our theory of literary change, since the sample examined is generally conceded to be one of fairly low autonomy. Based on a model of logical propinquity, we should expect cultural variables to show higher correlations with the textual variables than do social variables.

Table 14.1 gives correlations between the major external and internal variables and Secondary Process imagery, the best index of regression for the English series. It is seen that the internal variables—psychopathology and time-in-series—yield the highest correlations. However, the cultural variables, with the exception of technological change, tend to be worse predictors than are the social variables; this is the reverse of what was expected. It can be argued that the correlations between technological change and external social stress and Secondary Process are spurious ones. Both technological change and external social stress are correlated

TABLE 14.1

Correlations between Secondary Process
Imagery and External and Internal
Independent Variables ($N = 21$;
One-tailed Tests of Significance)

Variable	Secondary Process
Idealism	.15
Materialism	−.09
Ethics of principles	.36*
Ethics of happiness	.00
External social stress	.58**
Internal social stress	−.05
Technological change	−.53**
Time-in-series	−.60**
Psychopathology	−.62*

Note. Correlations involving Psychopathology are biserial; all other correlations
are Pearson product-moment.
   * $p < .05$.
  ** $p < .01$.

highly with time, but in different directions. Since time-in-series
exhibits *higher* correlations with Secondary Process than do either
of the other variables, it is more tenable to argue that the
correlations involving external forces are spurious, rather than vice
versa.

DIRECTION OF RELATIONSHIPS

The theory does not deal with specific external variables.
Rather, other theories based on such variables are accepted as
partially valid. However, since the data are at hand, and since the
external variables were picked to have some logical relationship to
regressive imagery, it is of interest to examine predictions from
other viewpoints. One would expect negative relationships
between Secondary Process content in poetry and materialism,
ethics of happiness, and technological change. All four of these
can be seen as symptoms of modern breakdown of tradition. One
would expect positive relationships between Secondary Process
content in poetry and idealism and ethics of principles for the
above reasons and also from a cultural consistency model: ethics
of principles and idealism could be seen as being based upon

secondary process and superego dominance. A case could be made for saying that social stress leads either to increased withdrawal (and, thus, to increased regression) or to increased outward orientation (and, thus, to decreased regression) on the part of the poet. In other chapters we have espoused the second view and argued that such stress may lead to a reduction in the functional autonomy of the poetic system.

Table 14.1 contains correlations which tend to uphold the predictions regarding the cultural variables. The predictions concerning social stress leading to an increased outward orientation are confirmed only in the case of external social stress; but this set of correlations may be due to the fact that this variable is highly correlated with time. There is relatively little variation in internal social stress in the English series: this may account for the lack of clearcut relationships.

LEVEL OF INFLUENCE

One may ask how specific or direct is the influence exerted by external variables upon poetic content. Of course, there is no one answer to this question. Sometimes a work of art consists of a purposeful presentation or description of social events. Here the relationship is direct but of little significance, unless one wishes to infer social conditions from the work of art. In other cases, social events and structures condition the thought expressed in a work of art but are not directly dealt with. Table 14.2 presents correlations that both illustrate the complexity of such influences and tie up some of the issues raised in previous sections. In this table, correlations between selected tags and the external variables are presented.

First, let us examine the specificity of influence. One would expect that ethics of principles would be the best predictor of the tag Moral Imperatives, but while it is a significant predictor, it is far from being the best one. On the other hand, one might expect the social stress variables to be the best predictors of Aggression, but here the cultural variables tend to be much better. Replications of this pattern in other samples of poetry would be needed before making much of it, but it does point up the complexity of the problem.

We saw in the previous section that there was some evidence that external stress leads to a turning outward of the poet's attention. The correlations in Table 14.2 suggest that, at least in

TABLE 14.2

Correlations between Internal and External Variables and Selected Content Analysis Tags ($N = 21$; Two-tailed Tests of Significance)

Variable	Aggression	Chaos	Order	Moral Imperatives
Idealism	−.69***	−.17	.20	.09
Materialism	.62***	.26	−.04	−.14
Ethics of principles	−.39*	−.32	.29	.43*
Ethics of happiness	.56***	.28	.02	−.11
Technological change	−.32	.14	−.40*	−.50**
External social stress	−.25	−.45**	.22	.61***
Internal social stress	−.45**	−.32	−.07	−.18
Time-in-series	−.06	.20	−.48**	.56***

*p < .10.
**p < .05.
***p < .01.

this sample and with these variables, poetry seems to provide an escape mechanism, rather than an instrument of confrontation: Aggression and Chaos exhibit high *negative* correlations with the indices of social stress. In times of chaos, poetry speaks of order and avoids themes of chaos and aggression. But when the correlations are viewed in the context of the finding of increased outward orientation, and the high correlation between external social stress and Moral Imperatives, what is suggested is not so much escapism but a postulation of more desirable conditions which *ought* to prevail.

We have seen that, in regard to regressive imagery, internal variables seem to be slightly better predictors than are external ones. Even in cases of specific tags (e.g., Moral Imperatives), time-in-series is a better predictor than external variables which would logically be expected to be closely related to the tag. Since the series investigated is one with a low degree of autonomy, these findings, although tentative, lend further support to our theory.

Chapter 15
CONCLUSIONS AND PROSPECTS

Là, tout n'est qu'ordre et beauté.
BAUDELAIRE

SUMMARY

We confronted ourselves at the outset with the problem of artistic change and decided to concentrate on the case of change in poetry. After establishing the legitimacy of the problem as a subject for psychological inquiry, we suggested that, whatever else it must be, if it is to survive, a poem must in some sense be original as compared with previous poems. This constraint, mediated by the psychological laws governing the production of novel responses, ought to condition fundamentally the course of literary history. In order to develop this idea, we specified these psychological laws in some detail. We adopted as our model of the creative process Kris' formulation that the act of creation consists of an initial stage of regression, or cognitive dedifferentiation, and a subsequent stage of elaboration, entailing the use of mechanisms of a less regressed state of consciousness. According to our theory, the structural or stylistic aspects of poetry are more determined by the level of elaboration at which composition occurs, while content is more determined by the depth of regression at which "inspiration" occurs. We have shown that metaphor distance could

189

be increased by increases in depth of regression *or* by decreases in level of elaboration. Increases in depth of regression would be accompanied by increases in the frequency of regressive imagery in poetry, while decreases in level of elaboration would be accompanied by loosening and "disintegration" of poetic style, and decreases in regressive imagery. The average expected audience for poetry exerts more pressure against such stylistic disintegration than against increases in regressive content.

In Chapter 4, following a brief consideration of the sociology of the poetic system, the models of the psychology of creativity were applied to the problem of the history of poetry. We suggested that originality should be valued in a poetic system to the extent that the system is autonomous, or free of external controls and pressures. The value on originality should lead to attempts by poets to increase metaphor distance continually. This, in turn, should lead to cycles of increasing density of regressive imagery, punctuated by stylistic disintegrations (accompanied by decreases in regressive imagery). In a highly autonomous system, metaphor distance should exhibit a high rate of change, regression should reach greater depths, and stylistic change should be more far-reaching. Conversely, as autonomy is allowed to approach zero, all these changes should be damped down, and the theory should account for less and less of the variance in literary change.

Predictions from the theory were tested on the content analysis data and were generally substantiated. Incongruous Juxtapositions increased significantly as a function of time in the French series, while it tended to increase over time for the English series, but the trend did not reach significance. The rate of increase in the French series was higher than in the English, as was predicted on the basis of the French series' greater autonomy. Associative meaningfulness increased over time in both series, while variability in meaningfulness increased only in the French series. The findings of Cohen (1966) were seen as pointing in the same direction as ours concerning increases in incongruity in the French series. The sequence of stylistic changes in both series was as predicted, and stylistic change in both was indicated by statistically significant changes in the content analytic measures. In the English series, there was evidence that attempts were made to change style *via* changes in subject matter and surface style before structural change occurred. In the French series there seemed to be "stylistic slippage" due to continual increases in autonomy. Regressive imagery followed the predicted cyclic pattern in both series. However, changes in the English series, with some important exceptions, did not reach significance, while those for the French series did. In the French series it was clear that the individual regression categories reached peaks consistent with the level of regression they were intended to tap; over time, deeper and deeper levels of regression were reached. Changes in the average concreteness of poetic vocabulary were found to parallel the changes in regressive imagery. The general patterns found were, for the French series, increasing frequency of regressive imagery from ca. 1800 to ca. 1900 followed by stylistic disintegration accompanied by decreasing regression; for the English series, increasing regression from ca. 1700 to ca. 1760, followed by stylistic change and a new regressive cycle beginning ca. 1800. Regression reached much greater depths in the French series than in the English series. In the English series it showed up as decreases in the frequency of secondary process words, while in the French series the direct indices of primary process cognition also varied significantly. The conclusions concerning results for level of regression and for degree of stylistic elaboration are indicated schematically in Figure 15.1 (cf. Figure 3.1).

When the Regressive Imagery Dictionary is factor analyzed and the resultant factors rotated to approximate Osgood's semantic space, factor scores in both series exhibit significant and parallel trends; the trends were interpreted as being due to the words in the tags loading on the evaluation and the potency factors being "projective" and symbolic indices of regression. With these more subtle indices, the expected trends are found in the English as well as the French series. Variation in the level of regression at which the English poets were inspired was relatively slight, but it does conform to theoretical expectations. On the other hand, variations for the French series are more dramatic; they show up on the direct level in fluctuations of the regressive imagery and cross-sexual reference tags, as well as on the indirect level.

THE INDIVIDUAL POET

We have tended in our analyses to lump together poets, to look for mean values and long-term trends, rather than being interested in individual poets. It may be asked whether the theory applies within, as well as across, poets—i.e., whether poets strive continually to create productions more novel than their own previous poems, and whether increasing depth of regression is the method whereby this is accomplished. This question was put to an

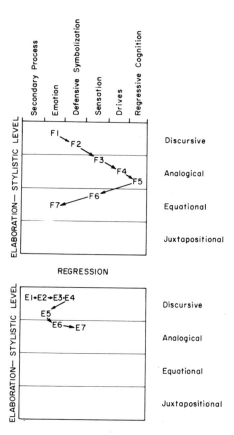

FIGURE 15.1 Interpretation of the findings for the French and English series.

empirical test. For such nonclassical poets (poets not in E1 or F1), as adequate chronologies by date of composition of texts were readily available, the fifty textual samples were divided at the median date of composition into an early and a late document for the poet. A chronology was considered readily available if it were present in a volume of texts otherwise meeting requirements for use in the study. In some cases, poems were arranged chronologically, but no dates were given; this presented no problem, since the first (in terms of the volume) twenty-five could be put in the early sample and the second in the late sample. If the theory is applicable within, as well as across, poets, then there should be more regressive imagery and Incongruous Juxtapositions in later than in earlier texts by the same poet, when the poet occupies a period where the theory predicts that increases in novelty are highly valued (i.e., all periods in our samples except E1 and F1).

Sums across subjects for the early and late documents were obtained and t-tests for related means were performed on the differences between early and late means. Incongruous Juxtapositions show no real trend over time (t = .20, ns). There is a consistent but generally insignificant tendency for the regressive imagery categories to *decrease* over the course of a poet's life. The fact that five of the six indices agree in showing decreased regression suggests that this is a real trend. Of the regression categories, only Drives increases. While the trend is consistent, it reaches significance only for Defensive Symbolization (t = -1.98, p = .06). At the same time, Being increases (t = 1.59, p = .13) while Analogy decreases insignificantly. The pattern of variation is similar to that found during periods F6 and F7, where a stylistic change entailing less elaboration and less regression was hypothesized to have occurred. Thus, there seems to be a slight tendency for poets to change along the stylistic, rather than the regressive, dimension vis-à-vis their own earlier productions.

Apparently, then, the theory of literary change is, at best, only marginally relevant to changes *within* any given poet's career. This is not altogether surprising, since there is a great deal of evidence that novelty is an important point of contention *across* generations and much less evidence that artists construe the norm for novelty as meaning that they must continually surpass their *own* performances. Were there more instances of the latter attitude, there would be more cases of older poets joining younger ones in rebellions against their own poetry. The rule seems to be that older poets defend, and continue writing in, their own style.

Another possible explanation can be based on the body of studies relating creative productivity to age. The general finding has been of a tendency toward early production of significant contributions with a falling off as age increases. There seems to be a sort of hardening of mental categories as one gets older. Within a depth psychological framework, such a decrement in creative ability could be related to a lessening capacity for regression. Within the arousal framework we have espoused, it could be tied to the fairly well-documented changes in average level of arousal with aging. More interesting is the possibility of curvilinear changes in level of regression over a poet's career. This may parallel the changes in level theoretically expected with the composition of an individual poem—i.e., increasing regression up to a point (corresponding to the inspirational phase of creation) and then decreasing regression (corresponding to the elaborational phase). Such a pattern would be congruent with Jung's concept of individuation: the process symbolized by descents into the unconscious/underworld and returns to the world with some treasure or rescued maiden, the process of integrating positive aspects of the unconscious with the conscious personality. In this view the poem reflects on a miniature scale, like the alchemical experiment, the life-course of the author; and, in this view, poetry would be seen as being in the service of self-knowledge or individuation. Such a view of the purpose of poetry is not at all inconsistent with the theoretical notion that poems are implicitly screened by author and critic on the basis of novelty. Nor is such a view beyond the scope of empirical investigation. With larger samples the hypothesis could easily be tested. It is probable that the hypothesis is overly simple. Poets who write for any length of time may run through several such cycles. Goethe, for example, seems to have exhibited a quite regular periodic alternation of regressive inspiration and barrenness.

We implied that, though novelty may be the ultimate and unbreachable value of the poetic system, individual poets may seek other goals in poetry. In large measure, the poet has no control over inspiration; it is something which comes over him from a seemingly alien sphere. This might be explained in terms of a structural variable such as the disinhibition or lack of control which seems to pervade all aspects of the behavior of the creative person (cf. Martindale, 1971). But the creative individual welcomes the regressive decomposition of his personality, which constitutes inspiration; he may even, by means of various drugs, seek to enhance it. Thus, it does make sense to ask what the artist seeks beyond novelty in such states. The concept of individuation is perhaps too inchoate to enter into an explanation, but it does give a clue to what the artist may be seeking. Many theorists have noted the feminine tinge to regressive states of consciousness. Individuation, according to Jung, is often symbolized in terms of the union of male and female figures. The poet may be a sort of psychic transsexual who is motivated to achieve regressive states of consciousness because of their feminine feeling tone (cf. Martindale, 1972b). Tendencies toward cross-sexual identification would seem to be important in understanding the creative personality. Ratings of the possibility of cross-sexual identification (based on, e.g., early father absence) were made on the poets in our sample. For the thirty-three poets for whom adequate biographical information was readily available, 55 percent exhibited a life history pattern suggesting the possibility of cross-sexual identification. Regressed states have, of course, other attributes besides a feminine tinge, and any of these could serve to draw an individual toward such states.

A study parallel to the one described in this book could be carried out, not on series of poetic texts, but on series of poets' personal documents. We have argued that the role of poet must change over time in any poetic system, to recruit personalities with the requisite need for novelty and capacity for regression. Such a study would derive predictions from what we know of the creative personality, rather than from what is known of the creative process. Where novelty must be attained by deeper and deeper regression, more and more regressive personality types would have to be recruited. For example, if a tendency toward cross-sexual identification covaries with inclination toward regression, we should expect it to become more and more blatant in the succession of poets recruited during a regressive phase; compare for example the "masculine protest" of the early romantics (e.g., Byron) with the effete characteristics of the later romantics (e.g., Wilde). On a more obvious level, degree of regression and degree of psychopathology tend to covary. We should expect more symptoms of pathology in poets during periods where deep regression is called for. Although we do not have enough cases to label these results as being other than tentative, the ratings of psychopathology used in the assessment of validity may be examined in this light. In general, we may predict that the middle periods (E3–E5 and F3–F5) should contain the highest proportion of pathological subjects since regressive imagery is maximal in these periods. Periods E1–E2 and F1–F2 should contain a low proportion because there is no need for deep regression, while periods E6–E7 and F6 F7 also call for less regression because of stylistic change. Table 15.1 shows that this prediction is confirmed at a significant level.

AN EXPERIMENTAL SIMULATION OF LITERARY CHANGE

Modern poetry has exhibited what might be called a romantic progression into the depths of the mind. The voyage begun by the romantic poets has continued without change in direction until the present day. The discontinuities, reactions, and counter-reactions in terms of which modern literary history is often seen

TABLE 15.1
Chi-Square Test on the Relationship between Psychopathology
and Time (Expected Values Are in Parentheses)

	Periods			
Pathology	1-2	3-5	6-7	N
1	(5.78)	(9.45)	(5.78)	
	10	6	5	21
2-3	(5.23)	(8.55)	(5.23)	
	1	12	6	19
N	11	18	11	40

$x^2 = 9.4$.
$p < .01$.

do not appear in our data; rather, romantic texts exhibit values intermediate between classic and Parnassian ones, Parnassian texts exhibit values intermediate between romantic and symbolist ones, and so on. Through the hazy imprecision we must live with at this early stage of scientific literary analysis, a profound order and regularity is evident. Whether or not we have explained this order correctly, clearly it could not possibly be the contingent product merely of larger social changes or of the chance appearance of men of genius. This belief is reinforced by evidence that modern literary history recapitulates, although on a different level, the pattern of past literary changes.

We have implied that de Stael's notion that art reflects society is analogous to Aristotle's belief that the rate of fall of an object is determined by its weight, that social influences are really influences on the order of friction which retard or introduce "noise" into a system, rather than being truly causal forces. Even if this be granted, one might argue that the "atmosphere" of art is so dense that the friction emanating from the larger society is often more important than the "gravity" we have identified with the need for novelty. We did, however, find evidence that even for the lower-autonomy English series, the theoretical independent variables were better predictors than indices of larger social and cultural changes. If this finding holds up in other contexts, it would imply that, even in low-autonomy artistic traditions, intrasystemic forces are more important than the larger society in shaping artistic products.

The data suggest orderly and predictable variations over time of regressive imagery, stylistic integration, metaphor distance, and the other variables investigated. Though these variations conform to theoretical expectations, we cannot be sure that they occurred for the reasons set forth in the theory. Perhaps some unsuspected variable highly correlated with the passage of time, which was used as an index of need for novelty, really accounts for the results. There are two ways in which this objection could be countered. First, studies of change in other artistic systems could be undertaken. Rather precise predictions could be made for a poetic series intermediate in autonomy between the French and the English ones, regardless of the larger social matrix from which the series was drawn. Chinese poetry of the T'ang Dynasty, late Roman poetry, and English metaphysical poetry were all probably written under conditions of autonomy intermediate between those of our series. Analogous patterns of change should be found in all these. As well, the increase in metaphor distance over time should be intermediate between that in the French and English series; cycles of regression should reach deeper levels than in the English series but not reach levels as deep as was the case with the French series. Such a cumulation of analogous patterns in diverse situations would lend credence to the idea that they arose from the intrapoetic, theoretically specified causes. A second approach would be to hold constant changes in the larger society by investigating change in parallel contemporary systems of differing autonomy—e.g., changes in the style and content of literary journals with high and low sales over the same span of time.

An alternate approach, and the one that was actually followed, would be to bring the phenomena into the laboratory, to experimentally manipulate the theoretical variables. On the face of it, the thought of experimentally simulating literary history sounds absurdly impossible. But the theory of artistic change is relatively simple, having to do with the induction of a need for novelty into a system that produces series of artistic responses. The purpose of this simulation, reported in Martindale (1973a), was to show that the theoretical variables are sufficient of themselves to produce changes of the sort observed in the content analytic study. If mere induction of the need for novelty into a poetic system produces changes of the kind that have occurred in literary history, then the law of parsimony requires us to regard other possible causal features as secondary.

The basic design was to seat ten highly creative subjects around a table and ask them to produce series of similes and Thematic Apperception Test stories, each of which had to be more original than preceding productions; after each response, papers were rotated, subjects read previous responses, a new response to the same stimulus was made by a different subject, and so on for ten trials. Two series of similes and one series of stories were produced. The series of responses in some ways remarkably paralleled the course of poetry over the last century. In two out of the three conditions the measure of metaphor distance increased significantly over trials. Regressive imagery varied as predicted in most cases. We found that induction of a higher need for novelty or restriction of possibilities for variation of a given style led to quicker increases in regressive imagery followed by rather clear stylistic disintegration, while a lower need for novelty or the existence of multiple possibilities for working out a style led to slower but continuous increases in regressive imagery with no stylistic disintegration.

In the TAT stories, the measure of metaphor distance, a variant of Incongruous Juxtapositions, increased significantly over trials. With regard to regressive imagery an interesting pattern was found when subjects were dichotomized into more- and less-creative groups. In the stories written by the less-creative group, the amount of regressive imagery increased continually and significantly over trials. However, for the more-creative group, amount of regressive imagery increased more quickly to a peak and then fell off dramatically. Examination of the later stories gave clear evidence that this decrease in regressive imagery was accompanied by stylistic change. For example, one subject switched from writing stories to drawing "cartoons" containing words, music, and pictures. Other subjects switched from a serious, dramatic style to an absurd one. The research of Houston and Mednick (1963) and others suggests that highly creative subjects have a greater need for novelty than do less-creative ones. The experimental induction of a need for novelty should, then, produce in such subjects a more powerful need to produce original responses. Theoretically, this should lead to a speeding up of the process of regression and stylistic disintegration. This, of course, is exactly what we found.

An analogous pattern was found with the similes data. With one set of similes, subjects were limited to responding with an adjective and a noun. No such restrictions were made with the other set. In the unrestricted set, with multiple opportunities for working out a style, there were continuous increases in regressive imagery over trials. In the restricted set, however, regressive imagery rose to a peak and then decreased. Again, the decrease in later trials was accompanied by indications of stylistic disintegration. Probably the clearest example of a stylistic shift is the series of responses to the stimulus, "A table is like _____":

1. the sea, quiet.
2. a horizontal wall.
3. a Formica'd bed.
4. the platonic form.
5. a dead tree.
6. a listening board.
7. versatile friendship.
8. vanquished forests.
9. a seasoned man.
10. two chairs.

The first three responses are based on the flatness of the surface of the table. The fourth response mediates these responses and the fifth and sixth responses, which base themselves on the material composition of tables. This is a shift in subject matter but does not disrupt the level of elaboration. Rather, it could be argued that composition is a slightly more distant associative category than is shape. The level of elaboration is such that responses not relevant to the physical attributes of a table are filtered out. However, this filtering device is *discarded* after trial 7, which appears to be arbitrary and idiosyncratic, but is probably based upon associations to the sixth response: only a disintegration in stylistic level permits such a response. In this context, the eighth response represents a relative failure; however, the last two responses establish the new style. The ninth response is evidently mediated by the word *seasoned*, which is transferred from wood to man. Although the associative source of the response is evident, a higher level of elaboration would have led to its rejection since a table is not objectively like a man. The two merely share, in different senses, a common attribute. The tenth response relies on the close associative relationship of table and chair. This, in the context of low elaboration, overrides the objective dissimilarity of the two objects: again there is contiguity but *not* similarity. Such a response would not have been possible on the initial level of elaboration.

We do seem to find clear examples of stylistic or structural disintegration in the late similes of restricted length. For purposes of comparison, let us examine some examples from the other series. There is a tendency here for later responses to be associatively distant rather than to be the products of stylistic disintegration (which allows inappropriate combinations of close associates). This is evident in the series of responses to the stem,

"A pencil is like _____":

   1. a yellow cigarette, spreading its cancer on paper.
   2. the headwaters of a river, flowing from the mind to the world.
   3. a black light on nothing.
   4. a stiletto, piercing truth.
   5. an artist's brush, painting paper.
   6. an ice-scraper, unfreezing one's view of the world.
   7. the scratchy fingernails of an insomniac.
   8. a grenade: useful, destructive, yet often self-destructive.
   9. the neck of an hourglass.
10. God micturating upon the cosmos.

The hypothesis is illustrated by the difference between the fourth and the ninth responses. Both of these seem to be mediated by shape: a stiletto is obviously "closer" to the shape of a pencil, but the neck of an hourglass does not strike us as being a product of such extreme low elaboration as some of the late restricted length responses. This view is reinforced by the possibility that it is based not only on shape but also on an unconscious concretization of the thought expressed in the second response (the neck of the hourglass connects its two halves just as the river—or pencil—connects the mind and the world). The same thought is concretized as well in the tenth response:

   2. (the headwaters of) a river flowing (from the) mind (to the) world.
10.   micturating   [by]   God (upon the) cosmos.

It is the parallels between the ninth and tenth and earlier responses which show that the later ones are in reality physiognomic and concrete expressions of the ideas expressed in the earlier ones. The earlier similes are metaphoric while the later are more hypnogogic in character, but both express the "reasonable" idea that a pencil is used for communication. The later responses are regressive, concrete, and distant rather than products of the low elaboration–low regression syndrome. Significantly, the eighth simile seems arbitrary in its basic form ("a pencil is like a grenade") but is explained. Surely the addition of such an explanation is the work of a high level of elaboration.

The same physiognomic expression occurs in the last response to "Pride is like _____":

10. a green tumor swelling from the bottom of the brain, which inhibits thought and increases the size of the head, eventually splitting the skull and emerging as a stalk of celery.

The simile seems to represent a low level of elaboration. But note that it is in reality two responses: one is the cliché "Pride is like having a swelled head," while the other is an original physiognomic and concrete apprehension of this cliché: "*Pride* is like a green tumor which *swells* and splits *the head* and emerges as a stalk of celery." This response is not based on associative contiguity, but rather on distant associates representing a comprehensible idea. It is explained and it makes sense: images filtered through a high level of elaboration always make sense, although it may be an arcane sort of sense, while those not so filtered need not make sense.

The series of responses listed here shows in miniature what occurs in the history of poetry. Metaphor distance increases and, with it, regressive imagery, indicating the regressive sources of the increasingly novel similes. But, as is seen with the similes of restricted length and the stories composed by the more creative subjects, eventually the limits of regression are reached and style must disintegrate if the orderly expansion of metaphor distance is to continue. Highly similar patterns are thus found in laboratory simulation and in historical reality.

Whatever one wishes to conclude in regard to the theory, it seems clear that the methods used in assessing it are fruitful. We have experienced no particular difficulties in content-analyzing poetry or even in bringing it into the laboratory. Trends were not, as the skeptic might have thought, completely swamped by variance. Although, in the main, the quantitative data yield conclusions roughly similar to what could be claimed from qualitative examinations, they offer much more precision and are more likely to be believed. Further, they show up the profound and beautiful regularity of the history of the literary series we have examined, to an extent that would have been impossible with qualitative descriptions.

REFERENCES

Albrecht, M. C. The relationship of literature and society. *American Journal of Sociology*, 1956, *59*, 425-436.

Alpert, M. *Perceptual determinants of affect.* Unpublished M.A. thesis, Wesleyan University, 1953.

Alvarez, A. *The school of Donne.* London: Chatto and Windus, 1961.

Aragon, L. *Le paysan de Paris.* Paris: NRF, 1926.

Arieti, S. *The intrapsychic self: Feeling, cognition, and creativity in health and mental illness.* New York: Basic Books, 1967.

Auden, W. H. Squares and oblongs. In C. D. Abbott (Ed.), *Poets at work.* New York: Harcourt Brace Jovanovich, 1948.

Bachelard, G. *La poétique de la reverie.* Paris: Presses Universitaires de France, 1960.

Barron, F., & Welsh, G. S. Perception as a possible factor in personality style: Its measurement by a figure preference test. *Journal of Psychology*, 1952, *33*, 199-207.

Bateson, G., Jackson, D. D., Haley, J., & Weakland, J. Toward a theory of schizophrenia. *Behavioral Science*, 1956, *1*, 251-264.

Baudelaire, C. Fusées. In *Oeuvres complètes.* Paris: NRF, 1961. (Original dates, 1855-1862.)

Baudelaire, C. Mon coeur mis à nu. In *Oeuvres complètes.* Paris: NRF, 1961. (Original dates, 1859-1866.)

Berlyne, D. E. The influence of complexity and novelty in visual figures on orienting responses. *Journal of Experimental Psychology*, 1958, *55*, 289-296.

Berlyne, D. E. *Conflict, arousal, and curiosity.* New York: McGraw-Hill, 1960.

Berlyne, D. E. *Structure and direction in thinking.* New York: Wiley, 1965.

Berlyne, D. E. Arousal and reinforcement. In D. Levine (Ed.), *Nebraska Symposium on Motivation* (Vol. 15). Lincoln: University of Nebraska Press, 1967.

Berlyne, D. E. Novelty, complexity and hedonic value. *Perception and Psychophysics*, 1970, *8*, 279-286.

Berlyne, D. E. *Aesthetics and psychobiology.* New York: Appleton-Century-Crofts, 1971.

Berlyne, D. E., Craw, M. A., Salapatek, P. H., & Lewis, J. L. Novelty, complexity, incongruity, extrinsic motivation and the GSR. *Journal of Experimental Psychology*, 1963, *66*, 560-567.

Berlyne, D. E., & Crozier, J. B. Effects of complexity and prechoice stimulation on exploratory choice. *Perception and Psychophysics*, 1971, *10*, 242-246.

Berlyne, D. E., Koenig, J. D. V., & Hirota, T. Novelty, arousal, and the reinforcement of diversive exploration in the rat. *Journal of Comparative and Physiological Psychology*, 1966, *62*, 222-226.

Berlyne, D. E., & Parham, L. C. Determinants of subjective novelty. *Perception and Psychophysics*, 1968, *3*, 415-423.

Bernard, O. (Ed. and trans.). *Rimbaud.* Baltimore: Penguin, 1966.

Blake, W. Letter to Thomas Butts. In A. G. B. Russell (Ed.), *The Letters of William Blake.* London: Methuen, 1906. (Original date, 1803.)

Blum, G. S. *A model of the mind.* New York: Wiley, 1961.

Bogen, J. E. The other side of the brain: An appositional mind. *Bulletin of the Los Angeles Neurological Societies*, 1969, *34*, 135-162.

Breton, A. *Manifeste du surréalisme.* Paris: NRF, 1963. (Original date, 1924.)

Breton, A. *Second manifeste du surréalisme.* Paris: NRF, 1963. (Original date, 1929.)

Bruner, J. S., Goodnow, J. J., & Austin, G. A. *A study of thinking.* New York: Wiley, 1956.

Brunetière, F. *Evolution de la poésie lyrique au XIXe siecle.* Paris: Hachette, 1894.

Cassirer, E. *The philosophy of symbolic forms.* New Haven: Yale University Press, 1955. (Original date, 1925.)

Chambers, F. *Cycles of taste.* Cambridge: Cambridge University Press, 1928.

Chomsky, N. Some methodological remarks on generative grammar. *Word*, 1961, *17*, 219-239.

Cohen, J. *Structure du langage poétique.* Paris: Flammarion, 1966.

Colby, B. N. Development and applications of an anthropological dictionary. In P. J. Stone et al., *The general inquirer: A computer approach to content analysis.* Cambridge, Mass. M.I.T. Press, 1966.

Combarieu, J. *Histoire de la musique*. Paris: Flammarion, 1913.

Connors, C. Visual and verbal approach motives as a function of discrepancy from expectancy level. *Perceptual and Motor Skills*, 1964, *18*, 457–464.

Couch, A. J. *Data-text system: A computer language for social science research*. Unpublished preliminary manual, Harvard University, 1967.

Croker, J. W. Review of "Endymion: A poetic romance." *The Quarterly Review*, 1818, *19*, 204–208.

Day, H. I. Looking time as a function of stimulus variables and individual differences. *Perceptual and Motor Skills*, 1966, *22*, 423–428.

Day, H. I. Evaluation of subjective complexity, pleasingness and interestingness for a series of random polygons varying in complexity. *Perception and Psychophysics*, 1967, 2, 281–286.

Deonna, W. *L'archéologie, sa valeur, ses méthodes* (3 vols.). Paris: H. Laurens, 1912.

Dinkel, T. *Psychoactive drug dictionary*. Cambridge, Mass.: Cambridge Computer Associates, n.d.

Dunham, H. W. Epidemiology of psychiatric disorders as a contribution to medical ecology. *International Journal of Psychiatry*, 1968, *5*, 124–146.

Durkheim, E. *Suicide*. Glencoe, Ill.: The Free Press, 1951. (Original date, 1897.)

Ehrenzweig, A. *The psycho-analysis of artistic vision and hearing*. New York: Braziller, 1965. (Original date, 1953.)

Ehrenzweig, A. *The hidden order of art*. Berkeley: University of California Press, 1967.

Eliot, T. S. *Selected essays, 1917–1932*. New York: Harcourt, Brace, 1932.

Empson, W. *Seven types of ambiguity*. London: New Directions, 1930.

Engel, R. Experimentelle Untersuchungen über die Abhängigkeit der Lust and Unlust von der Reizstärke beim Geschmacksinn. *Archiv für die gesamte Psychologie*, 1928, *64*, 1–36.

Escarpit, R. *Sociology of literature*. Painesville, Ohio: Lake Erie College Studies, 1965. (Original date, 1958.)

Evans, D. R. *Conceptual complexity, arousal and epistemic behaviour*. Unpublished Ph.D. thesis, University of Toronto, 1969.

Fenichel, O. *The psychoanalytic theory of neurosis*. New York: Norton, 1945.

Fiedler, K. *On judging works of visual art*. Berkeley: University of California Press, 1949.

Fischer, J. L. Art styles as cultural cognitive maps. *American Anthropologist*, 1961, *63*, 79-93.

Fischer, R. A cartography of the ecstatic and meditative states. *Science*, 1971, *174*, 897-904.

Fitzgerald, E. T. Measurement of openness to experience: A study of regression in the service of the ego. *Journal of Personality and Social Psychology*, 1966, *4*, 655-663.

Flatter, R. *Shakespeare's producing hand, a study of his marks of expression to be found in the first folio.* London: W. Heinemann, 1948.

Foçillon, H. *The life of forms in art.* London: Wittenborn, 1942.

Fowlie, W. *Mallarmé.* Chicago: University of Chicago Press, 1953.

Fowlie, W. (Ed. and trans.). *Mid-century French poets.* New York: Grove Press, 1959. (Original date, 1955.)

Fowlie, W. *Climate of violence: The French literary tradition from Baudelaire to the present.* New York: Macmillan, 1967.

Franz, M. -L. von (Ed.). *Aurora consurgens.* New York: Bollingen, 1966.

Freud, S. The interpretation of dreams. In A. A. Brill (Ed.), *Basic writings of Sigmund Freud.* New York: Modern Library, 1938. (Original date, 1900.)

Freud, S. Psychopathology of everyday life. In A. A. Brill (Ed.), *Basic writings of Sigmund Freud,* New York: Modern Library, 1938. (Original date, 1904.)

Freud, S. Wit and its relation to the unconscious. In A. A. Brill (Ed.), *Basic writings of Sigmund Freud.* New York: Modern Library, 1938. (Original date, 1905.)

Freud, S. The relation of the poet to daydreaming. In *Collected papers* (Vol. IV). New York: Basic Books, 1960. (Original date, 1908.)

Gamble, K. R., & Kellner, H. Creative functioning and cognitive regression. *Journal of Personality and Social Psychology*, 1968, *9*, 266-271.

Gardner, H. (Ed.). *The metaphysical poets.* Baltimore: Penguin Books, 1957.

Gautier, T. *Mademoiselle de Maupin.* Paris: Editions Garnier Frères, 1955. (Original date, 1835.)

Ghiselin, B. (Ed.). *The creative process.* New York: Mentor, 1964. (Original date, 1952.)

Giles, H. A. *A history of Chinese literature.* New York: Grove Press, n.d. (Original date, 1923.)

Gill, M., & Brenman, M. *Hypnosis and related states.* New York: International Universities Press, 1959.

Goldstein, K. *The organism.* Boston: Beacon Press, 1939.

Gombrich, E. H. Review of *Social history of art* by A. Hauser. *Art Bulletin*, 1953, *35*, 79–84.

Gombrich, E. H. Psychoanalysis and the history of art. In B. Nelson (Ed.), *Freud and the twentieth century*. New York: Meridian, 1956.

Graña, C. *Bohemian versus bourgeois: French society and the French man of letters in the nineteenth century*. New York: Basic Books, 1964.

Grosse, E. *The beginnings of art*. New York: D. Appleton, 1893.

Haber, R. N. Discrepancy from adaptation level as a source of affect. *Journal of Experimental Psychology*, 1958, *56*, 370–375.

Hankiss, E. The structure of literary evolution. *Poetics*, 1972, *5*, 40–66.

Harding, R. *An anatomy of inspiration*. New York: Barnes and Noble, 1967. (Original date, 1940.)

Hartley, A. (Ed.). *The Penguin book of French verse*. Vol. 4, *The Twentieth Century*. Baltimore: Penguin, 1959.

Hartley, A. (Ed.). *Mallarmé*. Baltimore: Penguin, 1965.

Hauser, A. *The social history of art*. London: Routledge and Kegan Paul, 1951.

Hayward, J. *The Oxford book of nineteenth century English verse*. London: Oxford University Press, 1964.

Haywood, H. C. Novelty-seeking behavior as a function of manifest anxiety and physiological arousal. *Journal of Personality*, 1962, *30*, 63–74.

Hazard, P. *Quatre études*. New York: Oxford University Press, 1940.

Hegel, G. W. F. *The philosophy of fine art* (4 vols.) London: G. Bell, 1920. (Original date, 1835.)

Hempel, C. G., & Oppenheim, P. Studies in the logic of explanation. *Philosophy of Science*, 1948, *15*, 135–175.

Herdan, G. *The advanced theory of language as choice and chance*. New York: Springer-Verlag, 1966.

Hines, D., & Martindale, C. Functional brain asymmetry, primary process thinking and natural language. *Electroencephalography and Clinical Neurophysiology*, 1973, *34*, 773. (Abstract) (a)

Hines, D., & Martindale, C. *Creativity and the operant control of the alpha rhythm*. Paper presented at Eastern Psychological Association Convention, Washington, D.C., 1973. (b)

Holland, N. *The dynamics of literary response*. New York: Oxford University Press, 1968.

Holsti, O. External conflict and internal consensus: The Sino-Soviet case. In P. J. Stone et al., *The general inquirer: A computer approach to content analysis.* Cambridge, Mass.: M.I.T. Press, 1966.

Holt, R. *Manual for the scoring of primary process manifestations in Rorschach responses.* New York: Research Center for Mental Health, New York University, 1968.

Housman, A. E. *The name and nature of poetry.* Cambridge: Cambridge University Press, 1933.

Houston, J. P., & Mednick, S. A. Creativity and the need for novelty. *Journal of Abnormal and Social Psychology,* 1963, *66,* 137–141.

Johnson, S. *The lives of the most eminent English poets* (4 vols.). London: J. Rivington and Sons and others, 1790–1791. (Original dates, 1779–1781.)

Jones, A., Wilkinson, J. H., & Braden, I. Information deprivation as a motivational variable. *Journal of Experimental Psychology,* 1961, *62,* 126–137.

Jones, W. T. *The romantic syndrome.* The Hague: Martinus Nijhoff, 1961.

Jung, C. G. Psychology and alchemy. *Collected works* (Vol. 12), New York: Pantheon, 1956. (Original date, 1944.)

Jung, C. G. Mysterium coniunctionis: An inquiry into the separation and synthesis of psychic opposites in alchemy. *Collected works* (Vol. 14), New York: Pantheon, 1956.

Jung, C. G. The archetypes and the collective unconscious. *Collected works* (Vol. 9, Pt. I), New York: Pantheon, 1959.

Kahler, E. *The disintegration of form in the arts.* New York: Braziller, 1968.

Kahler, E. *The inward turn of narrative.* Princeton, N. J.: Princeton University Press, 1973.

Kalin, R., Davis, W. N., & McClelland, D. C. The relationship between use of alcohol and thematic content of folktales in primitive societies. In P. J. Stone et al., *The general inquirer: A computer approach to content analysis.* Cambridge, Mass.: M.I.T. Press, 1966.

Kalin, R., McClelland, D. C., & Kahn, M. The effects of male social drinking on fantasy. *Journal of Personality and Social Psychology,* 1965, *1,* 441–452.

Kamman, R. Verbal complexity and preferences in poetry. *Journal of Verbal Learning and Verbal Behavior,* 1966, *5,* 536–540.

Kaplan, A., & Kris, E. Esthetic ambiguity, In E. Kris, *Psychoanalytic explorations in art.* New York: International Universities Press, 1952. (Original date, 1948.)

Kassebaum, G. C., Couch, A. S., & Slater, P. The factorial dimensions of the MMPI. *Journal of Consulting Psychology*, 1959, *23*, 226-236.

Kavolis, V. *Artistic expression—A sociological analysis.* Ithaca, N.Y.: Cornell University Press, 1968.

Klinger, E. *Structure and functions of fantasy.* New York: Wiley, 1971.

Kratin, G. [Analysis of "indifferent" stimuli from the electro-encephalogram in man], *Fiziologichesky Zhurnal SSSR*, 1959, *45*, 16-23.

Kris, E. *Psychoanalytic explorations in art.* New York: International Universities Press, 1952.

Kroeber, A. Configurations of culture growth. Berkeley: University of California Press, 1944.

Kučera, H., & Francis, W. N. *Computational analysis of present-day American English.* Providence: Brown University Press, 1967.

Leckart, B. T. Task specific decrements in the duration of attention. *Psychonomic Science*, 1967, *9*, 559-560.

Leckart, B. T., Briggs, B., & Kirk, J. Effect of novelty on stimulus selection in children. *Psychonomic Science*, 1968, *10*, 139-140.

Lehmann, A. *Hauptgesetze des menschlichen Gefühlslebens.* Leipzig: Reisland, 1892.

Levey, H. B. A theory concerning free creation in the inventive arts. *Psychiatry*, 1940, *3*, 229-293.

Lévy-Bruhl, L. *How natives think.* New York: Washington Square Press, 1910.

Lindsley, D. B. Attention, consciousness, sleep and wakefulness. In J. Field (Ed.), *Handbook of Physiology.* Sec. 1. *Neurophysiology* (Vol. 3). Washington, D.C.: American Physiological Society, 1960.

Lomax, A. *Folk song style and culture.* Washington, D.C.: American Association for the Advancement of Science, 1968.

Lucas, St. J., & Jones, P. M. *The Oxford book of French verse.* London: Oxford University Press, 1957.

Ludwig, A. Altered states of consciousness. In C. Tart (Ed.), *Altered states of consciousness.* New York: Wiley, 1969.

Lukács, G. *Studies in European realism.* New York: Grosset and Dunlap, 1964.

Maher, B. The language of schizophrenia: A review and interpretation. *British Journal of Psychiatry*, 1972, *120*, 3-17.

210 REFERENCES

Mannheim, K. *Ideology and utopia.* New York: Harvest Books, 1964. (Original date, 1936.)

Maritain, J. *Creative intuition in art and poetry.* Cleveland: Meridian, 1965. (Original date, 1953.)

Martin, L. C. (Ed.). *The poems, English, Latin, and Greek of Richard Crashaw.* London: Oxford University Press, 1957.

Martin, L. J. An experimental study of Fechner's principles of aesthetics. *Psychological Review,* 1906, *13,* 142-219.

Martindale, C. *The psychology of literary change.* Unpublished Ph.D thesis, Harvard University, 1969.

Martindale, C. Degeneration, disinhibition, and genius. *Journal of the History of the Behavioral Sciences.* 1971, ,7, 177-182.

Martindale, C. Father absence, psychopathology, and poetic eminence. *Psychological Reports,* 1972, *31,* 843-847. (a)

Martindale, C. Femininity, alienation, and arousal in the creative personality. *Psychology,* 1972, *9,* 3-15. (b)

Martindale, C. An experimental simulation of literary change. *Journal of Personality and Social Psychology,* 1973, *25,* 319-326. (a)

Martindale, C. *The semantic significance of spatial movement in narrative verse.* Paper presented at International Conference on Computers in the Humanities, Minneapolis, 1973. (b)

Martindale, C. *Primitive mentality and the relationship between art and society.* Paper presented at V International Colloquium on Empirical Aesthetics, Leuven, 1973. (c)

Martindale, C. Approximation to natural language, grammaticalness, and poeticality. *Poetics,* 1974, *9,* 21-25. (a)

Martindale, C. *The psychophysiology of creativity.* Paper presented at American Psychological Association Convention, New Orleans, 1974. (b)

Martindale, C. *Regressive imagery in schizophrenic letters.* Unpublished research, University of Maine, 1974. (c)

Martindale, C., Abrams, L., & Hines, D. Creativity and resistance to cognitive dissonance. *Journal of Social Psychology,* 1974, *92,* 317-318.

Martindale, C., & Armstrong, J. The relationship of creativity to cortical activation and its operant control. *Journal of Genetic Psychology,* 1974, *124,* 311-320.

Martindale, C., & Greenough, J. The differential effect of increased arousal on creative and intellectual performance. *Journal of Genetic Psychology,* 1973, *123,* 329-335.

Martindale, C., Hasenfus, N., & Kinney, D. *The effect of instructions to be original on EEG patterns.* Unpublished research, University of Maine, 1973.

Martindale, C., & Hines, D. Right occipital alpha rhythm in high and low creative subjects during intelligence and creativity testing. *Electroencephalography and Clinical Neurophysiology*, 1973, *34*, 772. (Abstract) (a)

Martindale, C., & Hines, D. *Linguistic features in the speech of a case of Gilles de la Tourette's syndrome*. Paper presented at X International Congress of Neurology, Barcelona, 1973. (b)

Martindale, C., Reynes, R., & Dahl, H. *Lexical differences between working and resistance sessions in psycholanalytic therapy*. Paper presented at Society for Psychotherapy Research Meeting, Denver, 1974.

Maslow, A. H. Two kinds of cognition and their integration. *General Semantics Bulletin*, 1957, *20*, 17–22.

Maslow, A. H. *Toward a psychology of being*. Princeton, N.J.: Van Nostrand, 1962.

McClelland, D. C. French national character and the life and works of André Gide. In D. C. McClelland, *The roots of consciousness*. Princeton, N.J.: Van Nostrand, 1963.

McClelland, D. C., Atkinson, J. W., Clark, R. A., & Lowell, E. L. *The achievement motive*. New York: Appleton-Century-Crofts, 1953.

McKellar, P. *Imagination and thinking*. New York: Basic Books, 1957.

McReynolds, P. Exploratory behavior as related to anxiety in psychiatric patients. *Psychological Reports*, 1958, *4*, 321–322.

Mead, G. H. *Mind, self, and society*. Chicago: University of Chicago Press, 1934.

Mednick, S. A. A learning theory approach to schizophrenia. *Psychological Bulletin*, 1958, *55*, 316–327.

Mednick, S. A. The associative basis of the creative process. In M. T. Mednick and S. A. Mednick (Eds.), *Research in personality*. New York: Holt, Rinehart, and Winston, 1963.

Metraux, R., et al. *Some hypotheses about French culture*. New York: Research in Contemporary Cultures, Columbia University, 1950.

Meyer, L. B. *Emotion and meaning in music*. Chicago: University of Chicago Press, 1956.

Michaud, G. *Introduction à une science de la littérature*. Istanbul: Matbassi, 1950.

Miles, J. *Eras and modes in English poetry*. Berkeley: University of California Press, 1957.

Miller, G. A., & Selfridge, J. A. Verbal context and the recall of meaningful material. *American Journal of Psychology*, 1950, *63*, 178–185.

Mitchell, B. R., & Deane, P. *Abstract of British Historical Statistics*. Cambridge: Cambridge University Press, 1962.

Munsinger, H. L., & Kessen, W. Uncertainty, structure and preference. *Psychological Monographs*, 1964, *78*(9, Whole No. 586).

Neisser, U. *Cognitive psychology*. New York: Appleton-Century-Crofts, 1967.

Neumann, E. *The origins and history of consciousness*. New York: Bollingen, 1954.

Nietzsche, F. The birth of tragedy from the spirit of music. In *The philosophy of Nietzsche*. New York: Modern Library, 1927. (Original date, 1872.)

Noble, C. E. An analysis of meaning. *Psychological Review*, 1952, *59*, 421-430.

Nordau, M. *Degeneration* (5th ed.). London: William Heinemann, 1895.

Ogilvie, D. M. The Icarus complex. *Psychology Today*, 1968, *3* (7), 30-34, 67.

Ortega y Gasset, J. *The dehumanization of art*. Garden City, N.Y.: Doubleday, 1956. (Original date, 1948.)

Osgood, C. E. Motivational dynamics of language behavior. In M. R. Jones (Ed.), *Nebraska Symposium on Motivation* (Vol. 5). Lincoln: University of Nebraska Press, 1957.

Osgood, C. E., Suci, G. J., & Tannenbaum, P. H. *The measurement of meaning*. Urbana: University of Illinois Press, 1957.

Paivio, A., Yuille, J. C., & Madigan, S. Concreteness, imagery, and meaningfulness values for 925 nouns. *Journal of Experimental Psychology Monograph Supplement*, 1968, *76* (1, Pt. 2).

Peckham, M. *Man's rage for chaos: Biology, behavior, and the arts*. Philadelphia: Chilton, 1965.

Pfaffman, C. The pleasures of sensation. *Psychological Review*, 1960, *67*, 253-268.

Piaget, J. *The psychology of intelligence*. New York: Harcourt, Brace, 1950.

Pine, F. A manual for rating drive content in the Thematic Apperception Test. *Journal of Projective Techniques*, 1960, *24*, 32-45.

Pine, F., & Holt, R. R. Creativity and primary process: a study of adaptive regression. *Journal of Abnormal and Social Psychology*, 1960, *61*, 370-379.

Plekhanov, G. *Art and society*. New York: Critics Group, 1936. (Original date, 1913.)

Poggioli, R. *The theory of the avant-garde*. Cambridge, Mass.: Harvard University Press, 1968.

Poincaré, H. *The foundations of science*. Lancaster, Pa.: The Science Press, 1913.

Pound, E. *Make it new: Essays*. New Haven: New Directions, 1934.

Praz, M. *The romantic agony*. Cleveland: Meridian, 1963. (Original date, 1933.)

Praz, M. Review of *Shakespeare's imagery* by C. Spurgeon. *English Studies*, 1936, *18*, 177–181.

Provins, K. A. Environmental heat, body temperature and behaviour: An hypothesis. *Australian Journal of Psychology*, 1966, *18*, 118–129.

Rapaport, D. Cognitive structures. In J. E. Bruner et al., *Contemporary approaches to cognition*. Cambridge, Mass.: Harvard University Press, 1957.

Raymond, M. *De Baudelaire au surréalisme*. Paris: Librairie Jose Corti, 1963. (Original date, 1940.)

Read, H. *In defence of Shelley and other essays*. London: Heinemann, 1936.

Reitlinger, G. *The economics of taste: The rise and fall of the picture market, 1760–1960*. New York: Holt, Rinehart, and Winston, 1961.

Reverdy, P. *Le gant de crin*. Paris: Plon, 1926. (Original date, 1918.)

Reynes, R. *Variations in regressive imagery during psychoanalytic therapy*. Unpublished Ph.D. thesis, University of Maine, 1974.

Riegl, A. *Spätrömische Kunstindustrie nach den Funden in Osterreich-Ungarn*. Vienna: Staatstruckerei, 1927. (Original date, 1901.)

Roget's International Thesaurus. New York: Thomas Y. Crowell, 1962.

Roheim, G. *Magic and schizophrenia*. Bloomington: University of Indiana Press, 1955.

Rosenberg, H. *The tradition of the new*. New York: McGraw-Hill, 1959.

Russell, W. A., & Jenkins, J. J. *The complete Minnesota norms for responses to 100 words from the Kent-Rosanoff association test*. University of Minnesota studies on the role of language in behavior, Technical Report No. 11, 1954.

Sartre, J. -P. *Baudelaire*. Paris: Librairie Gallimard, 1950.

Schachter, S. *The psychology of affiliation*. Stanford, Calif.: Stanford University Press, 1959.

Schneirla, T. C. An evolutionary and developmental theory of biphasic processes underlying approach and withdrawal. In M.

R. Jones (Ed.), *Nebraska Symposium on Motivation* (Vol. 7). Lincoln: University of Nebraska Press, 1959.

Schücking, L. L. *The sociology of literary taste.* Chicago: University of Chicago Press, 1966. (Original date, 1923.)

Shannon, C. E., & Weaver, W. *The mathematical theory of communication.* Urbana: University of Illinois Press, 1948.

Sharpe, E. F. Certain aspects of sublimation and delusion. *International Journal of Psychoanalysis*, 1930, *11*, 12–23.

Shattuck, R. (Ed. and trans.). *Apollinaire: Selected writings.* New York: New Directions, 1948.

Shroder, M. Z. *Icarus: The image of the artist in French Romanticism.* Cambridge, Mass.: Harvard University Press, 1961.

Shumaker, W. *Literature and the irrational.* New York: Prentice-Hall, 1960.

Siegel, S. *Nonparametric statistics for the behavioral sciences.* New York: McGraw-Hill, 1956.

Silberer, H. On symbol-formation. In D. Rapaport (Ed.), *Organization and pathology of thought.* New York: Columbia University Press, 1951. (Original date, 1912.)

Skaife, A. M. *The role of complexity and deviation in changing taste.* Unpublished Ph.D. thesis, University of Oregon, 1967.

Smith, D. N. *The Oxford book of eighteenth century verse.* London: Oxford University Press, 1965. (Original date, 1926.)

Sokolov, E. N. *Perception and the conditioned reflex.* New York: Macmillan, 1963.

Solomon, P., & others. *Sensory deprivation.* Cambridge, Mass.: Harvard University Press, 1961.

Sorokin, P. A. *Social and cultural dynamics* (4 vols.). New York: American Book Company, 1937. (Abridged version, Boston: Porter Sargent, 1957.)

Spurgeon, C. *Shakespeare's imagery and what it tells us.* Cambridge: Cambridge University Press, 1935.

Stael, G. de. Literature considered in its relation to social institutions. In M. Berger (Ed.), *Madame de Stael on politics, literature, and national character.* Garden City, N.Y.: Doubleday, 1964. (Original date, 1800.)

Stone, P. J., Dunphy, D. C., Smith, M. S., Ogilvie, D. M., & associates. *The general inquirer: A computer approach to content analysis.* Cambridge, Mass.: M.I.T. Press, 1966.

Stone, P. J., & Kirsch, J. *User's manual for the general inquirer.* Cambridge, Mass.: M.I.T. Press, 1968.

Taine, H. *History of English literature.* New York: Grosset and Dunlap, 1908. (Original date, 1863.)

Tillich, P. *Systematic theology*. Chicago: University of Chicago Press, 1967.

Venturi, R. *Complexity and contradiction in architecture*. New York: Museum of Modern Art, 1966.

Vitz, P. C. Preference for different amounts of visual complexity. *Behavioral Science*, 1966, *11*, 105–114.

Vitz, P. C. Preference for tones as a function of frequency (Hz) and intensity (db). *Perception and Psychophysics*, 1972, *11*, 84–88.

Wells, H. W. *Poetic imagery*. New York, 1924.

Werner, H. *Comparative psychology of mental development*. New York: International Universities Press, 1948.

Wild, C. Creativity and adaptive regression. *Journal of Personality and Social Psychology*, 1965, *2*, 161–169.

Williamson, G. *The Donne tradition*. New York: Noonday Press, 1958. (Original date, 1930.)

Wölfflin, H. *Renaissance and baroque*. Ithaca, N.Y.: Cornell University Press, 1967. (Original date, 1888.)

Wright, G. T. The lyric present: Simple present verbs in English poems. *Publications of the Modern Language Association of America*, 1974, *89*, 563–579.

Yule, G. U. *The statistical study of literary vocabulary*. Cambridge: Cambridge University Press, 1944.

Zajonc, R. B. Social facilitation. *Science*, 1965, *149*, 269–274.

Zuckerman, M., Kolin, E. A., Price, L., & Zoob, I. Development of a sensation-seeking scale. *Journal of Consulting Psychology*, 1964, *28*, 477–482.

AUTHOR INDEX

Numbers in italics refer to the pages on which the complete references are cited.

SUBJECT INDEX